Herbert Puchta and Jeff Stranks

English in Mind

* Combo 1B · Student's Book

CAMBRIDGE
UNIVERSITY PRESS

	Unit	Grammar	Vocabulary	Pronunciation
Module 1 **Far and wide**	1 The languages we speak	Comparative adjectives Superlative adjectives	Language learning Everyday English	*than*
	2 We're going on holiday	Present continuous for future arrangements	Future time expressions Holiday activities	/θ/ *(think)* & /ð/ *(th...*
	3 What will happen?	*will/won't*	Expressions to talk about the future Everyday English	*'ll*
	4 Never give up!	*too* + adjective Adverbs	The weather	/əʊ/ *(go)*
	Module 1 Check your progress			
Module 2 **The things people do!**	5 Good intentions	*be going to* (intentions & predictions) *must/mustn't*	Phrasal verbs (2) Everyday English	*must* & *mustn't*
	6 You shouldn't do that!	*should/shouldn't* *What's it like?*	Personality adjectives Adjectives for expressing opinions	Silent consonants
	7 How brave!	First conditional *when* & *if*	Adjectives of feeling Everyday English	Stress in condition... sentences
	8 It's a mad world	Present perfect + *ever/never*	Animals Verb & noun pairs	*have* & *has* in the present perfect
	Module 2 Check your progress			

Projects ● Speaking exercises: extra material ● Workbook ● Grammar reference ● Wordlist

Speaking & functions	Listening	Reading	Writing
Comparing things	Descriptions & interview about language learning	More than one language Amazing facts – or just lies? Story: I have to bounce!	Description or letter/email about language learning
Talking about arrangements Discussing holiday plans	Dialogues about holiday plans	Welcome to Ireland Culture: Adventure holiday in paradise	Magazine article about a class trip
Making predictions Talking about your future life	Science fiction story Future predictions Song: Space Oddity	Dialogue from a science fiction story Story: How embarrassing!	Competition entry about your life in the future
Describing the weather Giving advice Describing actions	Dialogue about the life of Wilma Rudolph	We can't give up! Culture: New Americans	Email giving advice to a friend
Talking about intentions	Dialogue about New Year's resolutions Dialogue about an unlucky day	New Year's resolutions Story: A birthday party	Email about New Year's Eve
Giving advice & recommendations Planning a friend's visit	Information about different customs	Quiz: Other cultures Culture: Tips for the tourist in Britain	Letter/email giving tips to a tourist
Expressing future possibilities Telling a story	Dialogues about bravery	Face-to-face with a gorilla Story: Dave's risk	Re-telling a story about facing danger
Talking about life experiences Talking about things you've done / never done	Interview about strange pets	Have you ever seen anything like it? John Evans, the Headbalancer Culture: Elvis lives	Letter/email about a visit to Los Angeles

● Irregular verbs and phonetics

Module 1
Far and wide

YOU WILL LEARN ABOUT ...

- The world's best language learners ....
- Holidays in Ireland ....
- An adventure holiday ....
- A science fiction story ....
- Four young mountain climbers ....
- Europeans who went to live in America ....

  * Can you match each picture with a topic?

YOU WILL LEARN HOW TO ...

Speak
- Compare and contrast things
- Compare the lives of famous people
- Talk about your future arrangements
- Talk about your holiday plans
- Make predictions about your future life
- Describe your habits using adverbs
- Re-tell a story

Write
- A letter/an email about a language course
- A magazine article about arrangements for a class trip
- A competition entry about your life in the future
- An email giving advice to a friend

Read
- An article about language learners
- A web page about holidays in Ireland
- A tourist brochure about Ireland
- An article about arrangements for an adventure holiday
- A dialogue from a science fiction story
- An article about climbers in the Himalayas
- An article about Europeans going to live in the USA

Listen
- Teenagers talking about language learning
- A radio interview with a good language learner
- A dialogue about holiday plans
- A dialogue from a science fiction story
- Teenagers making predictions about their future
- A song about an astronaut
- A dialogue about the life of an athlete

Use grammar

Can you match the names of the grammar points with the examples?

Comparative adjectives

Superlative adjectives

Present continuous for future arrangements

will/won't

too + adjective

Adverbs

It **won't hurt**!

We can't do it – it's **too difficult**.

It's the **longest** river in the world.

They stood up **slowly**.

Pronunciation is **more difficult** than grammar.

We**'re visiting** Ireland next summer.

Use vocabulary

Can you think of two more examples for each topic?

Language learning	Future time expressions	Holiday activities	The weather
translate	tomorrow	sightseeing	sunny
have an accent	in two days' time	camping	foggy
....	....	....	....
....	....	....	....

1 The languages we speak

* Comparatives and superlatives
* Vocabulary: language learning

1 Read and listen

a The text is about a group of people. Who are they and why are they special? Read the text quickly to find the answers.

b 🔊 Now read the text again and listen. Mark the statements *T* (true) or *F* (false).

1 A lot of people in Florida speak Spanish as their first language. ☐

2 Some Vaupés River Indians only speak two languages. ☐

3 A Vaupés Indian can't marry someone who speaks the same language. ☐

4 The Vaupés Indians don't have a language that they all understand. ☐

c Do many people in your country speak more than one language? Which languages do people speak?

d One language in the world has more speakers than English. Which do you think it is?

Arabic   Chinese   Russian   Spanish

More than one language

It's not unusual to learn and use more than one language. In many countries around the world, almost everybody speaks more than one language. For example, in some parts of the USA (like Florida), a lot of people speak Spanish as their mother tongue. Most of these people learn English as well, and a lot of English speakers learn Spanish.

But perhaps the world's best language learners are the Indians who live near the Vaupés River in South America. About 10,000 of the Vaupés River Indians live in a small area of the Amazon rainforest. In this area, there are more than 20 completely different languages. All of the Vaupés River Indians speak three languages, often more than three. This is because when a person wants to get married, he or she has to marry someone who speaks a different language. So the children always learn three languages: their mother's first language, their father's first language and also Tukano, the language that all the Vaupés Indians have in common. Then when they are older, they have to marry someone who speaks a different language, and their children have to learn at least three languages. The number is often higher, as the Vaupés people often continue to learn more languages when they are teenagers and adults.

2 Listen

a 🔊 Roberto and Gabriela are talking about the languages they are learning. Listen and read.

b 🔊 Listen again and fill in the names of the languages.

Roberto (from Italy)
First language: Italian
Learning Spanish, German

Gabriela (from Argentina)
First language: Spanish
Learning English, Portuguese

Roberto:
My .... is good – it's better than my ....
Of course, for me .... is easier than ....
That's because it's got a lot of words that are almost the
same as .... The grammar is very similar, too.

Gabriela:
.... pronunciation is difficult for me. But of course
.... pronunciation is more difficult! I never know
how to pronounce a new word, because the writing and
the pronunciation are often very different.

3 Grammar
Comparative adjectives

a Underline examples of comparisons in the texts in
Exercise 2. Then complete the table.

	Adjectives	Comparative form
short adjectives (1 syllable)	long short big	long**er** *shorter* .... big**ger**
adjectives ending in -*y*	easy happy	 happ**ier** than ...
longer adjectives (2 or more syllables)	difficult important	**more** difficult ....
irregular adjectives	bad good far	worse .... further

b Complete the comparisons. Choose the correct adjective and use the comparative form.

1 Italian is *more modern than*
   (old / modern) Latin.
2 The Amazon River is ....
   (short / long) the Nile.
3 The Amazon rainforest is
   .... (big / small) India.
4 For most Europeans, learning
   Chinese is ....
   (easy / difficult) learning Italian.
5 Sydney is ....
   (close to / far from) my
   country .... Paris.

4 Pronunciation
than

a 🔊 Listen to the sentences
and underline the stressed
syllables.

1 Pronunciation is more
   difficult than grammar.
2 Spanish is easier than German.
3 My speaking is better than
   my writing.
4 Is French more interesting
   than English?

b 🔊 How do you pronounce
than? Listen again and repeat.

5 Speak

Work with a partner. Compare the
things in the list. Use adjectives
from the box or other adjectives
that you know.

interesting   good   beautiful
exciting   friendly   clean
nice   intelligent   easy
important   quiet   boring

1 CD-ROMs / books
2 summer / winter
3 football / tennis
4 dogs / cats
5 cities / villages
6 Spanish / German

6 Listen

(a) 🔊 Listen to the first part of a radio interview with Matthew Dawson. Fill in the first column of the table with the names of the languages.

(b) 🔊 Listen again. Tick (✓) where/how Matthew learned each language.

(c) 🔊 Matthew now talks about how to be a good language learner. Read the ideas in the list. Then listen and tick (✓) the ideas Matthew talks about.

1 Read and listen a lot.

2 Exchange emails or letters with a penfriend who speaks the language.

3 Think of ideas to test yourself when you're learning new words.

4 Listen to cassettes and imitate the pronunciation.

5 Make friends and practise speaking with people who speak the language.

6 Try not to make mistakes, but don't worry about them.

(d) Which ideas in Exercise 6c do you follow? Which ideas would you like to try?

Language	From his parents	In the country	At school in England	Taught himself
1 _English_	✓			
2 _____				
3 _____				
4 _____				
5 _____				

7 Vocabulary

Language learning

(a) 🔊 Check that you understand these words about learning and speaking languages. Then listen, check and repeat.

> make mistakes
> imitate   corrects
> translate   look up
> ~~have an accent~~
> means   guess
> communicate

(b) Read the text. Fill in the spaces with the words/ phrases from Exercise 7a.

Advice for language learners

It can sometimes be a little difficult to learn a foreign language. But there are many things you can do.

When you speak a foreign language, it's normal to ¹ _have an accent_ . It's OK – other people can usually understand. It's a good idea to listen to cassettes and try to ² _____ other speakers, to make your pronunciation better.

If you see a new word and you don't know what it ³ _____ , you can sometimes ⁴ _____ the meaning from words you know, or you can ⁵ _____ the word in a dictionary.

A lot of good language learners try not to ⁶ _____ things from their first language. Translation is sometimes a good idea, but try to think in the foreign language if you can!

It's also normal to ⁷ _____ . When your teacher ⁸ _____ a mistake in your writing or speaking, think about it and try to see why it's wrong. But it's more important to ⁹ _____ , so don't be afraid to speak!

8 Grammar

Superlative adjectives

a Read the sentences on the cards. Two of them aren't true. Which do you think they are?

1 The worst language learner lives in England. He started learning French ten years ago, but he can only say 30 French words.

2 The most common word in English is *the*.

3 The easiest language in the world is spoken in Tranquili in Africa. It only has about 1,000 words and there isn't any grammar.

Amazing facts – or just lies?

4 The continent with the most languages is Africa. There are more than 1,000 different languages in Africa.

5 The shortest place names only have one letter. In France there is a place called Y, and U is a place in the Caroline Islands in the Pacific.

6 The best examples of surprising words for *mother* and *father* come from the Georgian language in Central Asia. *Mother* is *deda* and *father* is *mama*.

7 The longest train station name in Britain has got 67 letters. It's a station in Wales called **GORSAFAWDDACHAIDRAIGODANHEDDOGLEDDOLLONPENRHYNAREURDRAETHCEREDIGION**.

b Cover the text. Can you answer these questions?

1 Which is the continent with the most languages?
2 What are the names of the places with the shortest names?
3 What is the most common word in English?

c Look at the table. Write the adjectives from the box in the second column. Then fill in the comparative and superlative forms.

> difficult   big   happy   fantastic   important

	Adjectives	Comparative	Superlative
short adjectives (1 syllable)	long short small	longer shorter	longest ....
short adjectives ending in 1 vowel + 1 consonant	.... fat	.... fatter	.... fattest
adjectives ending in -*y*	easy	easier	....
longer adjectives (2 or more syllables)	.... frequent	.... more frequent	.... most frequent ....
irregular adjectives	bad good many	worse better more	....

d Complete the sentences. Use the superlative form of the adjectives.

1 Many people say that Hungarian is one of the _most difficult_ (difficult) languages.
2 When Sarah won $1,000, she was the .... (happy) girl in the world.
3 The Internet was one of the .... (important) inventions in the 1960s.
4 Vatican City is the .... (small) country in the world.
5 When my grandmother died, it was one of the .... (bad) times in my life.
6 The Nile is the .... (long) river in the world.

I have to bounce!

9 Read and listen

a 🔊 Look at the photo story. What do you think *I have to bounce* means? Why do you think Lucy doesn't understand this expression? Read and listen to find the answers.

1

Amy: Bye, Lucy. I have to bounce!
Lucy: What?
Amy: I have to bounce. You know – I have to go. We say that a lot in San Francisco.

2

Lucy: That's cool! What other things do you and your friends say?
Amy: Well, for example, we say someone is 'sketchy' if we think they aren't very nice.
Lucy: Sketchy? All right! I like it.

3

Amy: What about things you say here in Britain?
Lucy: Well, if I say 'He's tasty', do you know what it means?
Amy: Beats me!
Lucy: It means he's good-looking.

4

Amy: Look, there's Dave. He's quite tasty, isn't he?
Lucy: Well, he's a bit sketchy sometimes – but I like him!
Dave: Hi! What are you two laughing about?
Amy: I can't tell you now – I have to bounce!
Dave: Huh?

b Mark the statements *T* (true) or *F* (false).

1 Amy says she has to go. ☐
2 Lucy doesn't like the word *bounce*. ☐
3 A *sketchy* person is someone who is very nice. ☐
4 Amy knows what *tasty* means. ☐
5 In Britain, *tasty* sometimes means 'good-looking'. ☐

10 Everyday English

In all languages, young people invent new words or give words new meanings. Look at the words that young people in Britain used for *good* between 1950 and 2000. What words or phrases are popular with teenagers in your country now?

11 Write

Do one of the two activities.

a Write about the languages you speak. Use the texts by Roberto and Gabriela on page 7 to help you.

b Imagine you are doing an English course at a language school in Britain or the USA. Write a letter or an email to an English-speaking friend. Think about these questions.

- Where are you writing from? (London? New York? Cambridge?)
- How do you like the English course?
- Who is your teacher?
- How many students are in your class? Where are they from?
- Is your English better now? How? (Is your grammar better? Do you know more words? Do you understand better?)

Start like this:

Dear .... *,*

I'm writing to you from [name of place]. *I'm doing an English course here. The course is ...*

For your portfolio

② We're going on holiday

✳ Present continuous for future arrangements
✳ Vocabulary: future time expressions, holiday activities

1 Read and listen

(a) Look at the web page with ideas for a holiday in Ireland.
Which ones do you think are good ideas for a holiday?

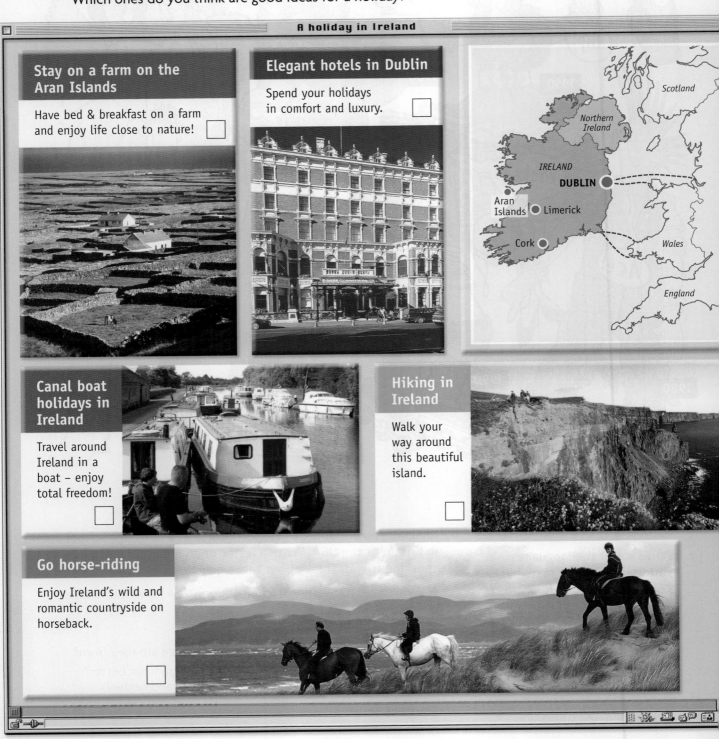

A holiday in Ireland

Stay on a farm on the Aran Islands

Have bed & breakfast on a farm and enjoy life close to nature!

Elegant hotels in Dublin

Spend your holidays in comfort and luxury.

Canal boat holidays in Ireland

Travel around Ireland in a boat – enjoy total freedom!

Hiking in Ireland

Walk your way around this beautiful island.

Go horse-riding

Enjoy Ireland's wild and romantic countryside on horseback.

(Map labels: Scotland, Northern Ireland, IRELAND, DUBLIN, Aran Islands, Limerick, Cork, Wales, England)

(b) 🔊 Listen to Kate and her brother, Greg. They are looking at the web page and planning their family's holiday. Number the activities 1–5 in the order you hear them in the dialogue.

c 🔊 Listen to Kate talking to her friend, Maggie, about the holiday plans. Complete the dialogue.

Maggie: Hey, Kate! How was your weekend?

Kate: Good! My brother and I planned the family summer holiday.

Maggie: Excellent! Where are you going?

Kate: We're ¹_____ to Ireland in August.

Maggie: Oh! How are you ²_____ there?

Kate: We're ³_____ by ferry. And we're ⁴_____ a week on a canal boat on the River Shannon.

Maggie: Great! Are you only ⁵_____ a week in Ireland?

Kate: No, two weeks. After the canal boat, we're ⁶_____ by train to Dublin and we're ⁷_____ in a really nice hotel there for two nights. And then we're ⁸_____ to the Aran Islands. We're ⁹_____ on a farm there.

Maggie: I think you'll have a great holiday! Are all your family ¹⁰_____?

Kate: Yeah. My dad says it's a bit expensive, but he's ¹¹_____ the bank manager tomorrow!

2 Grammar

Present continuous for future arrangements

a <u>Underline</u> examples of the present continuous in the dialogue for Exercise 1c.

We're spending a week on a canal boat.
Dad's seeing the bank manager tomorrow.

> **Rule:** We often use the present continuous to talk about plans and arrangements for the future.

b Complete the sentences.
Use the present continuous form of the verbs.

1 I _____ (visit) my grandparents in Rome next year.

2 Come to our place next Saturday. We _____ (have) a party.

3 Mum _____ (take) my sister to London on Thursday. They _____ (leave) early in the morning.

4 A: _____ you _____ (go) out tonight?
   B: No, I _____ (stay) at home.

5 My brother _____ (not come) on holiday with us this year. He _____ (work) in a shop for six weeks.

6 I've got toothache, so I _____ (see) the dentist tomorrow morning.

3 Vocabulary

Future time expressions

a Here are some expressions we can use to talk about the future. How do you say them in your language?

tomorrow

next week/Saturday/month/ weekend ...

in two/five days' time

the day after tomorrow

the week after next

b 🔊 Answer the questions. Then listen and repeat.

1 What day is the day after tomorrow?
   _____

2 What day is it in three days' time?
   _____

3 How many days is it until next Sunday?
   _____

4 What is the month after next?
   _____

4 Speak

Work with a partner. Tell him/her what you're doing:

- this evening
- tomorrow evening
- next Saturday
- next Sunday
- the weekend after next
- next July

A: *This evening I'm staying at home and watching TV.*

B: *I'm going to a restaurant with my parents tomorrow evening.*

1st January 2nd January

5 Read

(a) What do you know about Ireland? Read the questions and (circle) your answers. If you don't know the answers, guess them.

1 What is the capital of Ireland?
(Dublin) Limerick Cork

2 How many tourists visit Ireland every year?
about 1,000,000
about 2,000,000
about 5,000,000

3 How many people live in Ireland?
3,000,000
5,000,000
10,000,000

4 Which of these pop groups is Irish?
U2 UB40 5ive

(b) Now read the text. Check your answers to the questions in Exercise 5a.

(c) Find adjectives in the text to describe these things/people. Use a dictionary if you need to.

the people:
_warm_____, _____

the country:
_____, _____

the music:
_____

the hotels:
_____

the museums:
_____

Welcome to Ireland
– the perfect place for a holiday

About two million tourists visit the Republic of Ireland every year. They come from all over the world: Europe, Japan, and especially the United States of America, because many Americans have grandparents and great-grandparents who came from Ireland.

Why do so many people come to Ireland? Perhaps it's because the capital city, Dublin, has fascinating museums, comfortable hotels, and great restaurants. Or perhaps it's because the three million people who live in Ireland are so warm and friendly. Maybe it's because it's a charming and very beautiful country. But it's probably because of all of these things.

For young people, Ireland is a great place. Camping is easy, you can go windsurfing and canoeing, cycle around the island, or spend some time on a houseboat on one of the beautiful canals.

The music is exciting too. You can listen to traditional Irish music, or to the many great Irish pop groups. Sometimes, a lucky tourist sees Bono of U2 (the famous Irish band) walking down the street!

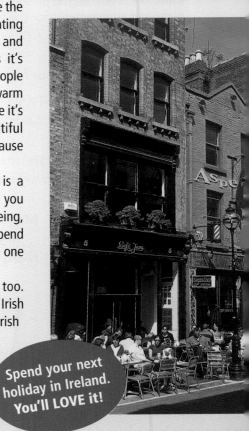

Spend your next holiday in Ireland. **You'll LOVE it!**

6 Vocabulary
Holiday activities

a 🔊 Write the names of the activities under the pictures. Then listen, check and repeat.

> canoeing   snorkelling   horse-riding   sailing   camping   sightseeing   windsurfing   sunbathing

1 _____

2 _____

3 _____

4 _____

5 _____

6 _____

7 _____

8 _____

b Work with a partner. Which of the activities do you like doing on holiday?

A: *I like windsurfing, but I'm not very good at it.*
B: *I don't like sunbathing. It's boring.*

c Fill in each space with a verb from the box.

> hire   travel   stay   buy   spend

1 _____ souvenirs / presents / postcards / stamps
2 _____ in a hotel / in a bed and breakfast / at a campsite / in a youth hostel / at home
3 _____ to Ireland / by ferry / by car / by plane / by train / by coach
4 _____ your holidays (in Ireland) / some time (on the beach) / two weeks (in Greece)
5 _____ a car / a boat / a bike / a surfboard

7 Speak

Work with a partner. Ask and answer about your plans for your next holiday.

Where / go / for your next holiday?
How / travel / there?   Where / stay?
How much time / spend there?   When / come back?

A: *Where are you going for your next holiday?*
B: *I'm going to ...*

8 Pronunciation
/θ/ (think) and /ð/ (that)

a 🔊 Listen and repeat the words.

1 think   three   month   something   toothache
2 that   those   with   brother   sunbathing

b 🔊 Listen and repeat the phrases. Underline *th* when the sound is /θ/. Circle *th* when the sound is /ð/.

1 Give me those things.
2 There's nothing in my mouth.
3 I think it's Thursday.
4 Your clothes are in the bathroom.
5 My mother thinks I'm crazy.
6 This month we're staying at a youth hostel.

Culture in mind

9 Read

a Where is Paul going for his next holiday? How long is he staying there? Read the text quickly to find the answers.

Adventure holiday in paradise

Paul Roberts (15) lives in New York. Like thousands of other American students, he usually goes away to a summer camp during the school holidays. These camps are just for teenagers, without their parents, and Paul always has a great time. But this summer he's doing something different – he's going on an adventure holiday in Hawaii. He tells us about his arrangements.

'It's a camping holiday for three weeks in Hawaii, for kids from 14 to 18. I'm leaving on 23rd July and coming back on 12th August.

'First, we're putting on backpacks and hiking through the jungle on an old native Hawaiian trail. They say it's incredibly beautiful, with huge waterfalls and spectacular beaches.

b Now read the text again. Tick the activities that Paul is doing on his holiday.

'After this five-day walk, we're staying for two days in a valley on the Pacific Ocean. The main activity here will be surfing. I don't know how to surf, but instructors will teach us how to do it, and I'm really looking forward to this.

'Then the organisers are providing mountain bikes and we're going for long rides – about 30 miles a day, around one of Hawaii's volcanoes. And on one day we're meeting a local Hawaiian family and helping them to plant fruit trees on their farm.

'After that, we're sailing for three days along the coast, and they say we'll have a chance to swim with dolphins and sea turtles! This sounds fantastic. Finally, we're going out for three days in sea kayaks – we're visiting sea caves and we'll be swimming and snorkelling too.

'Every night for the three weeks, we're camping in tents, usually on the beach. This isn't a holiday for couch potatoes! They say you have to be fit, and of course you have to know how to swim and ride a bike. But I think it's going to be a fantastic experience.'

c Mark the statements *T* (true) or *F* (false).

1 Paul usually spends the summer holidays with his parents. ☐
2 His adventure holiday is starting in July. ☐
3 People have to be 15 or older to go on this holiday. ☐
4 First, they are walking for five days. ☐
5 Paul is good at surfing. ☐
6 They are spending some time in a boat. ☐
7 They are sleeping in tents every night. ☐
8 Paul is feeling nervous about the holiday. ☐

d Would you like to go on the adventure holiday to Hawaii? Why / Why not?

10 Write

Imagine your class is going on a school trip for four days. Write an article for your school magazine about your arrangements. Include this information:

- where and when you are going
- which teachers are going
- how you are travelling there (by plane? by ferry? ...)
- where you are staying
- what you are doing there
- how long you are staying and when you are coming back

For your portfolio

(3) What will happen?

* will/won't
* Vocabulary: expressions to talk about the future

1 Read and listen

(a) Look at the picture of Samantha and Jake. Where are they?

(b) 🔊 Read and listen to the dialogue. Why are they frightened?

Samantha: Jake, we went into ¹_____ nearly two years ago and we're still looking for Planet Vulcan. What do you think? Will we find it?

Jake: Oh, yeah. I'm sure we will. Relax, Sam. The ²_____ is a big place, but we've got the computer to help us. We're in a new ³_____ now. Perhaps we'll find it here.

Samantha: OK, but I'm not sure about the computer. I know it's the most powerful computer in the world, but it tells terrible ⁴_____ .

Computer: Good morning, you lucky space travellers! This is your friendly computer speaking. Did you sleep well?

Samantha: Oh, hi, Bob. Yeah, fine, thanks. How about you?

Computer: Excellent! My last night of sleep was excellent.

Jake: Last night of sleep? What do you mean?

Computer: Oh, sorry, guys. Didn't I tell you? That red and blue ⁵_____ out there – can you see it? Our spaceship will ⁶_____ into it in exactly ... um ... one minute from now.

Jake: What? We can't! You have to do something!

Computer: Sorry! I'd like to help, but the ⁷_____ is out of control and there's nothing – I repeat, nothing – I can do. So in 45 seconds, we'll all be dead.

Samantha: Help! Do something!

Computer: I can't. But don't worry. When we die, in exactly ... um ... 30 seconds from now, it'll be very quick and it won't hurt! So I just want to say that I really enjoyed being with you on this spaceship. Thank you for being such good friends! 'We'll meet again, don't know where, don't know when ...'

b Write the holiday activities in the lists.

swimming   windsurfing   camping
horse-riding   sightseeing   snorkelling
canoeing   cycling   sunbathing   sailing

in/on water   not in/on water
swimming   ....

....

....

| 9 |

c Fill in the crossword with words to describe the weather.

1		2						3
s	n	o	w	i	n	g		
						4		
		5						
		6						
7								
8								

1➡ Look! It's .... The garden is white.

1⬇ It's .... outside. I'm going to sunbathe on the beach.

2   18° – it's .... today.

3   It's too .... to drive. We can't see the road in front of us.

4   It was very .... yesterday. A tree fell down in my street.

5   Take an umbrella. It's .... now.

6   It was .... yesterday. The temperature was 34°.

7➡ It's .... today. We can't see the sun.

7⬇ Come out of the sun. It's nice and .... under the trees.

8   Last night it was −10°. That's very .... !

| 9 |

3 Everyday English

Complete the dialogue with the words in the box.

embarrassing   the best bit
anything else   nonsense   cool
believe it

Lucy: A funny thing happened last week.

Teresa: What?

Lucy: Well, we went to a Chinese restaurant for a meal, and then we had fortune cookies.

Teresa: Oh, I love those.

Lucy: Me too. Mine said, 'Your life will be full of wonderful surprises!'

Teresa: Wow! That's [1] ___cool___ !

Lucy: Mum got a strange one. It said, 'You will have a lot of happiness if you stay happy.'

Teresa: Well, that's [2] .... ! It doesn't mean anything.

Lucy: Yes, I know. But [3] .... was when my dad ate his fortune cookie with the paper inside.

Teresa: Oh, no! I don't [4] .... !

Lucy: It's true! It was really [5] .... ! There were loads of people in the restaurant, and they all laughed.

Teresa: Did [6] .... happen?

Lucy: No, we paid the bill and left after that.

| 5 |

How did you do?

Tick (✓) a box for each section.

Total score	☺ Very good	😐 OK	☹ Not very good
54			
Grammar	18 – 24	13 – 17	less than 13
Vocabulary	18 – 25	14 – 17	less than 14
Everyday English	4 – 5	3	less than 3

Module 2
The things people do!

YOU WILL LEARN ABOUT ...

- New Year celebrations and resolutions ....
- Different cultures ....
- Tips for tourists in Britain ....
- A meeting with a gorilla ....
- Amazing records ....
- The fans of Elvis Presley ....

 Can you match each picture with a topic?

①

②

YOU WILL LEARN HOW TO ...

Speak
- Talk about your future intentions
- Give advice and recommendations
- Describe what things are/were like
- Talk about future possibilities
- Tell a story about a brave person
- Talk about experiences in your life

Write
- An email about your last New Year's Eve
- A letter/an email giving tips about your country
- The story of a film or a book
- A letter/an email about a visit to Los Angeles

Read
- A short text about New Year
- A dialogue about obligations
- A quiz about customs in different countries
- A brochure giving tourist tips about Britain
- A story about gorillas
- Short texts about amazing record-breakers
- An article about one of these record-breakers
- An article about the fans of Elvis Presley

Listen
- A dialogue about New Year's resolutions
- A dialogue about a teenager's unlucky day
- Short dialogues about customs in different countries
- A dialogue about bravery and risk
- An interview about strange pets

Use grammar

Can you match the names of the grammar points with the examples?

be going to	You **must** remember to feed the dog.
must/mustn't	I've **never been** to Paris.
should/shouldn't	I'm **going to** get fit.
What's it like?	If I **don't move**, he'll **go** away.
First conditional	What's the new girl **like**?
Present perfect + *ever/never*	You **shouldn't** arrive late.

Use vocabulary

Can you think of two more examples for each topic?

Phrasal verbs	Personality adjectives	Opinion adjectives	Animals
take up	hard-working	fantastic	rabbit
throw away	friendly	awful	snake
....	....	....	....
....	....	....	....

(5) Good intentions

✳ *be going to* (intentions and predictions), *must/mustn't*
✳ Vocabulary: phrasal verbs (2)

1 Read and listen

(a) How do British people celebrate New Year? Read the text to check your ideas.

(b) Find words or phrases in the text with these meanings.

1 the day before 1st January
   ---------------- ---------------- ----------------

2 12 o'clock at night
   ----

3 the time when it starts to get light in the morning

(c) 🔊 Listen to Mark and Annie talking about their New Year's resolutions. Write M (Mark), or A (Annie) next to each resolution.

Mark   Annie

1 I'm going to be more healthy. ☐
2 I'm going to take up scuba diving. ☐
3 I'm going to be more organised. ☐
4 I'm not going to eat chocolate. ☐
5 I'm not going to have arguments with my sister. ☐
6 I'm going to eat fruit every day. ☐

New Year's resolutions

It's 31st December – New Year's Eve. All over Britain, people are having parties, sometimes in their homes, sometimes out in the street. Ten seconds before midnight, the countdown begins:
10–9–8–7–6–5–4–3–2–1 ...
Happy New Year! Fireworks go off, and people kiss and stand in a circle to sing the old Scottish song *Auld Lang Syne*. They often keep up the celebrations until dawn.

Also at this time, people often begin to think about the year that is just starting. They think about the changes they're going to make and the things they're going to do in the new year. They make promises to themselves, called New Year's resolutions. But of course, people don't always stick to their resolutions!

2 Vocabulary
Phrasal verbs (2)

(a) 🔊 Match the verbs with the definitions. Then listen and repeat.

1 **take up** scuba diving   a put in the rubbish bin
2 **give up** chocolate   b start to do or learn
3 **throw away** my old papers   c continue
4 **work out** our problems   d stop doing something you enjoy
5 **keep it up**   e discover answers for

(b) Complete the sentences. Use the correct form of the phrasal verbs in Exercise 2a.

1 Last year my dad _gave_ _up_ smoking. He's a lot healthier now.
2 The Maths test was difficult, but I think I _____ _____ most of the answers.
3 Caroline loves sport. Three months ago she _____ _____ tennis and she's already very good at it.
4 I'm studying much harder now and I'm getting good results. I hope I can _____ it _____ !
5 Our old radio didn't work, so we _____ it _____ .

5 Pronunciation

Silent consonants

(a) 🔊 Listen and repeat the words. In each word, there is a 'silent' consonant which we don't pronounce. <u>Underline</u> the silent consonants.

1 honest 2 should 3 school
4 write 5 climb 6 know 7 two

(b) 🔊 Which consonants are silent in these words? Listen, check and repeat.

1 shouldn't 2 Thailand 3 foreign
4 listen 5 island 6 fascinating

(c) 🔊 Listen and repeat the sentences.

1 They should go to school.
2 I speak two foreign languages.
3 I know he's an honest person.
4 It's a fascinating island.
5 You shouldn't climb on the wall.

6 Grammar

What's it like?

(a) Match the questions with the answers.

1 What was the weather like on your holiday? ☐
2 What's your new teacher like? ☐
3 What are the people like in New York? ☐
4 What were the films like last night? ☐
5 What's this CD like? ☐

a They're very friendly and helpful.
b It's brilliant! You should listen to it.
c Well, I thought they were a bit boring.
d Awful! It rained all the time.
e She's nice and she's really funny!

(b) When we ask for an opinion about something or someone, we can ask: *What + be + subject + like?* Look at the questions in Exercise 6a and complete the table.

What	is	he / .... / it	
	....		.... ?
	....	they	
	were		

(c) Write the questions. Use the words in brackets.

1 A: I went to Greece last year.
   B: Really? What _____was it like_____ ? (it)
2 A: I've got the new Oasis CD.
   B: Oh? What _____ ? (it)
3 A: There's a new girl in our class.
   B: A new girl? What _____ ? (she)
4 A: We visited Spain a few weeks ago.
   B: Oh, that's nice! What _____ ?
   (the weather)
5 A: I've got some new trainers.
   B: Really? What _____ ? (they)
6 A: I read three books last week.
   B: Wow! What _____ ? (they)

7 Vocabulary

Adjectives for expressing opinions

(a) 🔊 Here are some adjectives we can use to give an opinion. Write them in the columns. Then listen, check and repeat.

~~boring~~ ~~brilliant~~ interesting attractive
fantastic awful cool dull ugly dreadful

+	−
brilliant _____	boring _____
_____	_____
_____	_____
_____	_____
_____	_____

(b) Which adjectives from Exercise 7a can you use to describe:

1 a film? 3 a city/town? 5 the weather?
2 a person? 4 a party?

8 Speak

Work with a partner. Ask and answer questions about the things in the box.

your brother/sister/parents/boyfriend/girlfriend
your town or city your home your last holiday
your favourite singer your last weekend

A: *What's your brother like?*
B: *He's OK sometimes. He's ...*

Culture in mind

9 Read

(a) Look at the title and the first two paragraphs of the text. What do you think the word *tips* means?

(b) Read the text. Match paragraphs 1–5 with the pictures. Write 1–5 in the boxes.

(c) Now read the text again. Then look at pictures a–e. Write sentences to explain what the people should and shouldn't do in Britain.

    a *She should look to the right.*

(d) Which of the things in the text are also true in your country?

Tips for the tourist in Britain

When you travel to a foreign country, you can see that the customs of the people there aren't always the same as yours. So before you go abroad, it's a good idea to find out something about the people who live in the country you're visiting.

The British are generally helpful and friendly but there are some things you should remember, so you don't make mistakes.

1 At bus stops, in cinemas and in shops, the British usually stand in queues. You shouldn't go to the front – you should stand in the queue and wait, like everyone else.

2 British people are usually polite and say *please* and *thank you* a lot. So when you're hungry, for example, you shouldn't say *I want a sandwich*. You should say *Can I have a sandwich, please?* When someone says *Thank you*, you can reply *You're welcome*.

3 When people say things you don't understand, you should say *Sorry?* or *Pardon?* and ask them to say it again. You shouldn't say *What?* – it isn't polite.

4 In some countries, people often kiss each other on the cheek when they meet. In Britain, you should only do this with people who are your friends or relatives. In formal situations, you should shake hands with the person.

5 Finally, don't forget – the British drive on the left. So before you cross the road, you should always look to the right!

10 Write

a Jill's penfriend, Mathilde, is visiting Britain in March.
Read Jill's letter and match the topics with the paragraphs.

a Things that Mathilde should/shouldn't do in Britain ☐

b Things that Mathilde should take to Britain ☐

c British people ☐

e Work with a partner. Make a list of useful tips for British tourists who are coming to visit your country.

I WANT THE SUGAR.

Hi Mathilde

I'm really happy you're coming to visit us here in Britain. I'm writing to tell you some things about my country.

1 First, I'm sure you're going to like the people here. They're usually friendly and helpful.

2 Remember to bring an umbrella and a raincoat. It often rains a lot in March and April. You should bring some warm clothes, too.

3 Don't forget, you should always say 'please' and 'thank you' when you ask for something. And you shouldn't go to the front of a queue — people hate that here!

I can't wait to see you!

Love,

Jill

b Imagine that your English-speaking penfriend is visiting your country soon. Write a similar letter or email to him/her.

For your portfolio

7 How brave!

* First conditional, *when* and *if*
* Vocabulary: adjectives of feeling

1 Read and listen

a How much do you know about gorillas? Mark the statements *T* (true) or *F* (false).

1 Gorillas live in families. ☐

2 Gorillas are dangerous and they often attack people. ☐

3 Gorillas will attack you if you show you're frightened, or if you run away. ☐

b Read the text quickly to check your answers in Exercise 1a.

c What is the text about? Choose one of the topics.

1 A woman who kills a gorilla

2 A woman who takes a baby gorilla back to its family

3 A family of gorillas and how they live

d 🔊 Now read the text again and listen. Answer the questions.

1 Why did the woman take the baby gorilla to the forest?

2 Why didn't the woman run away from the big gorilla?

3 Why did the big gorilla raise his hand?

4 Did the big gorilla take the baby gorilla?

e Find words in the text with these meanings.

1 the opposite of *ill* (paragraph 1) ....

2 know someone because you saw them before (paragraph 1) ....

3 moved up (paragraph 4) ....

f Do you think the woman in the text was brave? Why / Why not?

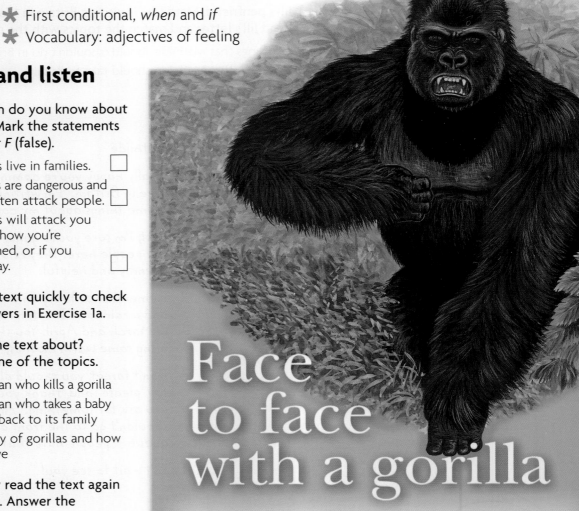

Face to face with a gorilla

I had found the baby gorilla four weeks before, and it was very ill. But now it was well again, and I had to take it back to its family. I picked it up, walked out to the car and drove to the forest. With the baby in my arms, I started to walk in among the trees. I was worried. 'If the mother doesn't recognise the baby, she won't take it back,' I thought. 'Perhaps she'll even kill it.'

The family was there. I put the baby gorilla down on the ground and walked a few metres away. Then I stopped and watched. I could see the mother looking at the baby, and I thought, 'Will she come closer? What will she do?'

Suddenly the father was there, in front of me. He was the biggest gorilla of the family. It was frightening because he was only a metre away. I was frightened, but I knew what to do. People think gorillas often attack people, but they don't – they only attack when you show you're scared. 'If I turn and run away, this gorilla will attack me,' I thought. 'But if I don't move, he'll go away.' I didn't move.

Suddenly the male gorilla lifted his hand. I was terrified. But he wanted to frighten me, not hit me. After a few seconds, he dropped his hand and turned. He went over to the baby, picked it up and moved away into the trees. I sat down on the ground. I was shaking.

2 Grammar

First conditional

a Match the two halves of the sentences. Check by looking back at the text on page 46.

1 If I turn and run away,
2 If the mother doesn't recognise the baby,
3 If I don't move,

a he'll go away.
b this gorilla will attack me.
c she won't take it back.

> **Rule:** We use the first conditional to talk about things we think are possible in the future.

b Complete the table.

If clause	Result clause	
If + present simple,	.... (will) .... (will not)	+ base form

c Put the words into the correct order to make the sentences.

1 see Jane / if / tell / I / I'll / her
----

2 my parents / I'm / will / if / late / be angry
----

3 I / bring it / I'll / to school tomorrow / if / remember
----

4 you'll / new friend, Jake / come / if / you / meet / my / to the party
----

5 rain tomorrow / if / the / it / doesn't / we'll / to / beach / go
----

6 the concert / if / tonight / I / don't / I / won't / feel better / go / to
----

d Complete the first conditional sentences with the correct form of the verbs.

1 If Kate ...*gives*... (give) me some help, I .... (finish) my homework in an hour.
2 You ....(not meet) anyone if you .... (not go out).
3 I .... (come) to your party if my mum .... (say) I can.
4 If Ken .... (not want) his ice cream, I .... (eat) it.
5 Susan .... (be) angry if she .... (hear) about this.
6 If we .... (buy) hamburgers, we .... (not have) enough money for the film.

3 Speak

Work with a partner.
Student A: Look at the questions below.
Student B: Turn to page 62.
Ask your questions and answer your partner's.

Student A

1 What will you do if it rains this weekend?
2 What will you do if the weather's nice?
3 How will you feel if your teacher gives you a lot of homework today?
4 What will you wear if you go out this evening?
5 What film will you see if you go to the cinema this week?
6 What programme will you watch if you watch TV this evening?

4 Pronunciation

Stress in conditional sentences

a 🔊 Listen to the sentences. Which words are stressed? Why, do you think? <u>Underline</u> the stressed words or syllables.

1 If it <u>rains</u>, I <u>won't go</u> to the <u>beach</u>.
2 We won't pass the test if we don't work hard.
3 I'll give him the card if I see him.
4 If you decide to come, I'll meet you at the cinema.
5 She won't arrive on time if she misses the train.
6 If he doesn't phone his parents, they'll worry about him.

b 🔊 Listen again and repeat.

5 Grammar

when and *if*

(a) What is the difference between sentences 1 and 2? Which speaker is sure he will see John?

1 *I'll give John your message when I see him.*
2 *I'll give John your message if I see him.*

(b) Complete the sentences with *if* or *when*.

1 I'm seeing Marta tomorrow. I'll ask her about the book _____ I meet her.

2 A: What are you doing tomorrow?
   B: _____ there's a good film on, I'll probably go to the cinema.

3 I'm not sure if I want to go to the disco tonight. But _____ I decide to go, I'll phone you.

4 It's too hot out in the sun now. Let's play tennis in the evening, _____ it's cooler.

6 Vocabulary

Adjectives of feeling

(a) Look at the examples from the text on page 46. Which adjective describes how the woman felt? Which adjective describes the situation?

*It was **frightening** because he was only a metre away.*
*I was **frightened**, but I knew what to do.*

(b) Underline other examples of *-ed* adjectives in the text on page 46.

(c) Write the adjectives under the pictures. Then listen, check and repeat.

| tired | bored | excited | interested | annoyed | frightened |

1 _____

2 _____

3 _____

4 _____

5 _____

6 _____

(d) Circle the correct adjective in each sentence.

1 I didn't like the film. I thought it was (boring) / bored.

2 I'm not at all *interesting / interested* in history. I prefer thinking about the future.

3 My friend, Elena, is really *frightening / frightened* of spiders. She can't stand them!

4 The football match was really *exciting / excited*. In the end Manchester United won 3–2.

5 The lesson wasn't very *interesting / interested*, so some of the students nearly fell asleep.

6 When I was younger I didn't like watching horror films. I found them too *frightening / frightened*.

7 My teacher was very *annoying / annoyed* when I told him I didn't have my homework.

8 I found the marathon really *tiring / tired* – I slept for 12 hours the next day!

7 Listen and speak

a Look at the pictures. Use a word from each box to label the people.

underwater	~~mountain~~		driver	fighter	jumper
racing	parachute	fire	photographer	~~climber~~	

1 *mountain climber*

2 _____

3 _____

4 _____

5 _____

b Which words can go with each picture? Write the words in the lists.

Nouns:
building parachute race ~~rope~~ shark

Verbs: attack burn ~~climb~~ collapse crash ~~fall~~ land open overturn swim

Picture 1	*rope*	*climb*	*fall*
Picture 2			
Picture 3			
Picture 4			
Picture 5			

c How brave do you think the people are? For each picture, write a score of 1–5 (1 = not very brave, 5 = extremely brave).

Picture 1 _____   Picture 2 _____
Picture 3 _____   Picture 4 _____
Picture 5 _____

d 🔊 Listen to Franco and Jenny. Which three pictures are they talking about? Complete the first column of the table.

	Franco	Jenny
Picture __5__	2	
Picture ____		
Picture ____		

e 🔊 Listen again. Write the scores that Franco and Jenny give to each person.

f Work with a partner. Talk about the scores you gave in Exercise 7c.

A: *What score did you give to the mountain climber? I gave her five. I think she's extremely brave.*

B: *I don't think so. I gave her two points because …*

Dave's risk

8 Read and listen

(a) 🔊 Look at the title and the photos. What do you think 'Dave's risk' is? Read and listen to find the answer.

Alex: You like Amy a lot, don't you?
Dave: Well, yeah, I do. She's lovely.
Alex: Does she like you too?
Dave: How should I know?
Alex: Ask her out, Dave. Then you'll know.

Maybe I *should* ask Amy to go out with me. But if she doesn't like me, she'll say no. Maybe she'll get angry. Then she won't want to be my friend any more!

Alex: So – did you ask her out?
Dave: No way!
Alex: Come on, Dave. She's a girl, not a monster.
Dave: Ha, ha.
Alex: Look, if you don't try, you'll never know, will you?

Dave: Um, Amy, I was thinking, maybe ... Would you like to go to the cinema tonight?
Amy: Oh, Dave. Sorry, no.
Dave: OK. No big deal. I'm sorry I asked.

Amy: No, Dave, hang on. It's just that today's my father's birthday. But I'd love to go tomorrow.
Dave: Really? Great! There's this old Mel Gibson film on, *Braveheart*. What about that?

(b) Mark the statements *T* (true) or *F* (false).

1 Dave likes Amy. ☐
2 Dave isn't sure how much Amy likes him. ☐
3 Alex isn't interested in Dave's problem. ☐

4 Dave doesn't want to lose Amy as a friend. ☐
5 Amy says she doesn't want to go to the cinema with Dave. ☐
6 Amy's dad doesn't want her to go out with Dave.

9 Everyday English

(a) Find expressions 1–4 in the photo story. Who says them? Match them with expressions a–d.

1 How should I know? a Wait.
2 No way! b No!
3 Hang on. c It isn't important.
4 No big deal. d I have no idea.

(b) How do you say expressions 1–4 in your language?

(c) Read the dialogues. Fill in the spaces with expressions 1–4 in Exercise 9a.

1 Julie: Come on, Mike. We have to leave now.
   Mike: _____ a minute. I'm just going to get my jacket.

2 Paolo: What time does the football match begin?
   Martina: _____ Why don't you ask Mario?

3 Tony: Can you lend me a pound?
   Simon: _____ You won't give it back, I know.

4 Judith: Sorry, I can't help you right now.
   Alice: _____ I'll do it myself.

10 Write

(a) Read what Geraldine wrote about a book she read. Answer the questions.

1 What was the book/film/programme?
2 Who was the main character?
3 Where was he/she?
4 Why was he/she in danger?
5 What did he/she do?
6 How did the story end?

The book I read is 'A Picture to Remember' by Sarah Scott-Malden. It's about a girl called Christina. One day, she saw two men in a car. One of them had a gun. They were bank robbers and she saw their faces. They didn't want her to tell the police, so they planned to kill her.

First, one of the robbers attacked her at the gym, but luckily she only hurt her arm. After this, she was in the street with her friend, Philippe, when one of the robbers drove his car into them. Philippe was hurt and had to go to hospital.

Christina went to visit Philippe. When she left the hospital in her car, the robbers followed her. Christina saw that they had a gun and understood that they wanted to kill her. She was frightened, but she kept calm. The robbers were close behind her, but they were driving too fast and couldn't stop. They crashed their car and it overturned. One of the robbers died and the police caught the other one.

(b) Write about a film, book or TV programme where somebody was in a dangerous situation. Use the questions and Geraldine's text to help you.

For your portfolio

8 It's a mad world

* Present perfect + *ever/never*
* Vocabulary: verb and noun pairs

1 Read and listen

(a) Read the texts quickly and match the paragraphs with the pictures.

Have you ever seen anything like it?

People have done some strange things to get into the record books! Here are some of them.

1 Len Vale Onslow is 103 years old. He's the oldest man in Britain with a licence to ride a motorbike, and he's never had an accident!

2 Hu Saelao, from Thailand, holds the world record for the longest human hair. His hair is 5.15 metres long – he's never cut it.

3 Strong man John Evans balances things on his head for ten seconds each time. At different times, John has balanced 62 books, 101 bricks, 548 footballs, even a Mini car!

4 Susan Smith, from Philadelphia, is probably the laziest woman on earth! The last time she got out of bed was 27 years ago.

5 Mel Ednie lives in Scotland, and he grows onions – big onions! He has broken the world record three times. In 1995, Mel grew an onion that weighed 7.2kg.

(b) 🔊 Now read the text again and listen. One of the texts is not true. Which one, do you think? (The answer is on page 57.)

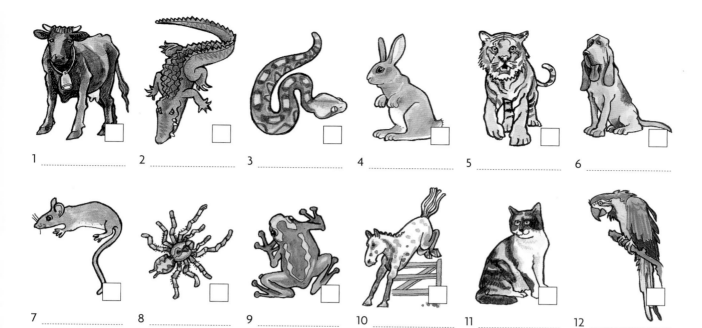

1 _____   2 _____   3 _____   4 _____   5 _____   6 _____

7 _____   8 _____   9 _____   10 _____   11 _____   12 _____

2 Vocabulary

Animals

🔊 Write the names of the animals in the pictures. Then listen, check and repeat.

> frog   horse   tiger
> rabbit   cow   parrot
> dog   alligator   mouse
> tarantula   cat   snake

3 Listen

a 🔊 Mr Brown wants to become a world record-holder. What record does he want? Listen to the first part of an interview with him to check your ideas.

Mr George Brown

b 🔊 Listen again and look at the pictures in Exercise 2. Tick the animals that Mr Brown has in his house.

c 🔊 Check that you understand the words in the box. Then listen to the second part of the interview and fill in the missing words.

> record   never   frogs   dangerous   woman   parrot   room

Interviewer: Is it difficult to have so many animals all in the same house?

Mr Brown: Sometimes. You see, I can't have the alligator in the same ¹_____ as the other animals. It's eaten some of the smaller ones. It loves ²_____ .

Interviewer: Yes, I see. So have you ever had any problems yourself? Some of these animals are ³_____ , aren't they?

Mr Brown: Well, the tarantulas have bitten me once or twice.

Interviewer: What do your neighbours think about all these animals?

Mr Brown: Well, they've ⁴_____ complained.

Interviewer: Have any of your pets ever escaped?

Mr Brown: Yes. The ⁵_____ escaped in 1998. But the alligator and the tarantulas have never escaped.

Interviewer: Oh, good! And tell me, Mr Brown, how many animals do you need to break the ⁶_____ ?

Mr Brown: Well, unfortunately, there's a ⁷_____ in America with more than 60 pets in her house, so I have a long way to go.

d Match the two parts of each sentence.

1	Mr Brown	a	have never complained about the pets.
2	The tarantulas	b	has escaped once.
3	The alligator	c	has had some problems with his pets.
4	His neighbours	d	has eaten several small pets in the house.
5	The parrot	e	have bitten him.

e Do you think Mr Brown is crazy? Why / Why not?

4 Grammar

Present perfect + *ever/never*

a) Look at the examples.
Complete the rule and the table.

*People **have done** some strange things.*
*John **has balanced** a Mini car on his head.*
*He's never **cut** his hair.*
***Have** you ever **seen** anything like it?*

Rule: We use the present perfect to talk about actions that happened some time up to now.

We form the present perfect with the present tense of .... + past participle.

Positive	Negative	Questions	Short answers
I/you/we/they 've (.............) worked	I/you/we/they **haven't** (**have not**) worked	.... I/you/we/they worked?	Yes, I/you/we/they **have**. No, I/you/we/they **haven't**.
he/she/it 's (.............) work**ed**	he/she/it 's (.............) work**ed**	.... he/she/it work**ed**?	Yes, he/she/it **has**. No, he/she/it **hasn't**.

b) Fill in the verb forms.
Use the Irregular verbs list on page 122 to help you.

Base form	Past participle
1 be	*been*
2 do	....
3 go	....
4 see	....
5 write	....
6 bite	....
7 speak	....
8 eat	....
9 drive	....
10 fly	....
11 swim	....
12 win	....

c) Complete the sentences. Use the present perfect form of the verbs.

1 We *'ve never lived* (never/live) in a foreign country.
2 .... she .... (ever/study) a foreign language?
3 I .... (never/see) a tarantula.
4 .... you .... (ever/drive) a car?
5 .... they .... (ever/fly) in a helicopter?
6 Jack .... (stay) in Japan, but he .... (never/eat) sushi.

5 Pronunciation

have and ***has*** in the present perfect

a) ◁)) Listen to the questions and answers.
How are *have* and *has* pronounced? Listen again and repeat.

A: *Have you ever driven a car?*
B: *Yes, I have.*
A: *Has she ever studied a foreign language?*
B: *Yes, she has.*

b) ◁)) Underline the stressed syllables. Then listen and repeat.

1 I've never lived in America.
2 Have you ever seen an alligator? No, I haven't.
3 Has he ever swum in a river? Yes, he has.

6 Speak

a) Work with a partner. Ask and answer the questions.

1 ever / see / a tiger?
2 ever / eat / Chinese food?
3 ever / be / on TV?
4 ever / speak / to a British person?
5 ever / win / any money?

A: *Have you ever seen a tiger?*
B: *No, never. Have you ever eaten Chinese food?*
A: *Yes, I have.*

b) Work with a partner or in a small group. Ask and answer about things you have done in your life. Use some of the verbs in the box.

travel	stay	play	win
eat	fly	drive	meet

b Complete the adjectives with the -ed or -ing ending.

1 I was really tir _ed_ last night when I went to bed. Yesterday was a very tir_____ day.

2 We were excit_____ about going to the football, but in the end it was a bor_____ match.

3 I thought the Dracula film was quite frighten_____ , but my girlfriend wasn't frighten_____ at all.

4 We went to a museum last Sunday. My parents thought it was fascinat_____ , but I wasn't really interest_____ .

| 7 |

c Find nine more animals in the wordsquare.

```
R  A  B  A  I  P  A  R  G  O
T  R  V  L  T  A  R  A  N  T
A  G  U  L  S  R  A  X  T  I
R  I  Q  I  L  R  O (D  O  G)
F  R  O  G  M  O  U  S  R  E
T  A  R  A  N  T  U  L  A  R
H  A  M  T  E  R  T  I  B  R
O  W  M  O  U  S  E  J  B  A
R  H  O  R  S  E  B  F  I  B
S  N  A  K  E  F  R  O  T  T
```

| 9 |

d Complete the sentences.
Use the correct form of the verbs in the box.

| raise   win   break   ~~build~~   tell   take |

1 My aunt and uncle are _building_ a house in the country at the moment.

2 I've been in a lot of competitions, but I've never _____ a prize.

3 If you want to succeed, you sometimes have to _____ risks.

4 People always laugh when Terry _____ a joke.

5 We're having a 'Fun Week' at school in October. We want to _____ money for sports equipment.

6 Joanna came first in her race and _____ the school record.

| 5 |

3 Everyday English

Complete the dialogues with the words in the box.

| It's no big deal   No way   ~~I'll pick up~~
How should I know   Hang on |

Carla: Matt, what are you doing next Saturday?

Matt: Saturday?

Carla: Yes. 4Tune are giving a concert, and I think it's going to be really good. If you like, ¹ _I'll pick up_ some tickets this afternoon, and then ...

Matt: ² _____ , Carla! Sorry, but I can't make it. I'm going to my grandparents' next weekend.

Carla: Oh, OK, that's fine. ³ _____ . I'll go with Ben and Lisa.

Matt: Sorry about that.

Carla: Do you like visiting your grandparents?

Matt: Yes, I do. Sunday lunch is the best bit. My granny cooks wonderful fish and chips.

Carla: Oh, Matt! How many calories are there in a plate of fish and chips?

Matt: ⁴ _____ ? I haven't got any idea.

Carla: Hundreds! If you eat that, you'll get fat.

Matt: No, I'll never get fat!

Carla: Are you sure? I can imagine you when you're 35 – big and fat!

Matt: ⁵ _____ ! That won't happen to me!

| 4 |

How did you do?

Tick (✓) a box for each section.

Total score	☺ Very good	☺ OK	☹ Not very good
67			
Grammar	27 – 36	20 – 26	less than 20
Vocabulary	20 – 27	15 – 19	less than 15
Everyday English	3 – 4	2	less than 2

Project 1

A poster about the future

1 Brainstorm

a You are going to make a poster and give a presentation about life in the future. Work in a group of four or five. In your group, decide on a topic that you all want to work on. For example:

- homes
- towns and cities
- transport
- schools
- clothes
- food
- communication
- weather
- something else

b In your group, decide how far into the future you want to look. Will you talk about the year 2025? 2100? 3000 ...?

c Think about what life will be like in the year you chose. For example, if you chose the topic *Food*, you can think about these questions:

- Will people eat healthy food?
- Where will their food come from?
- Will they eat more take-away meals?
- Do you think the food will be good to eat?
- Will it be more expensive?
- Will there be enough food for everybody?

Brainstorm ideas and make notes.

2 Make the poster

a Find or draw some pictures that fit with your ideas on the topic. For example, you can find photos from science fiction films in magazines or on the Internet, or you can draw your own pictures.

b Write short texts for each of the pictures you are going to use. For example:

> In the year 2050, robots will do the housework in most people's homes.

c At the top of your project paper, write the title of your presentation. For example:

> HOMES IN THE YEAR 2050

Arrange your pictures and short texts on the paper, but leave space at the bottom.

d At the bottom of the poster, write a longer text together. Say what you think about the future you are predicting. For example:

> Homes will be small, but they will be clean and comfortable. People will enjoy living at home because they won't have to do any housework.

3 Presentation

Present your poster to the other students in your class. Be ready to answer questions about it.

For your portfolio

Project 2
A talk on an event that happened this year

1 Listen

Listen to the beginning of three talks about memorable events that happened this year. What were the events?

2 Choose a topic

Spend some time thinking about the event that you will choose. Will you talk about an event that happened to you or an event that happened somewhere else in the world? Will you talk about something sad, something happy or something funny?

3 Plan

(a) Think about these questions:

- When and where did the event take place?
- Is there any background information that you will need to explain the event?
- What happened, exactly?
- Why was it memorable? How did you feel about it at the time? How do you feel about it now?

(b) Make a list of important words you will want to use. If you aren't sure of some words, look them up in a dictionary or ask your teacher. Then use the words to help you make notes for your talk. Don't write everything down in complete sentences – just write important phrases that will help you to remember what you want to say.

(c) Collect any information you need about your topic. If you can, collect pictures, drawings or photographs that might help you to make your talk more interesting.

(d) Practise your talk quietly to yourself.

4 Give the talk

Work in a group of four or five. Each student gives his/her talk to the others in the group. Be prepared to answer questions at the end of your talk.

For your portfolio

Speaking exercises: extra material

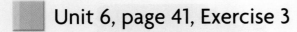

Unit 6, page 41, Exercise 3

Student B: Read the role card.
Take it in turns to listen to your partner's problem and give advice with *should* or *shouldn't*.

Student B

You love football and you love your favourite football team. But you have a problem. You are going to your best friend's birthday party on Saturday. But now you know that your team has an important match on Saturday, too. You want to see the match but you don't want to hurt your friend. Should you go to the match? Should you go to the party? Ask Student A.

Unit 7, page 47, Exercise 3

Student B: Look at the questions. Ask your questions and answer you partner's.

Student B

1 What will you do if you stay at home this weekend?
2 What will you study if you go to university?
3 What will you buy if you go shopping this weekend?
4 How will you feel if your parents ask you to do a lot of housework this evening?
5 Where will you travel if you go abroad on holiday this year?
6 Where will you go if you meet your friends tonight?

Thanks and acknowledgements

The authors would like to thank a number of people whose support proved invaluable at various stages of the planning, writing and production process of *English in Mind*:

Peter Donovan for inviting us do this exciting project for Cambridge University Press; Angela Lilley, Publishing Director at Cambridge University Press, for her leadership abilities and the support we got from her; James Dingle, our commissioning editor, for his commitment to the project, and for managing the editorial team; Annabel Marriott for her enthusiasm, her many excellent ideas and her commitment to quality in the editing of this course; Jackie McKillop for steering the course through its production.

The teenage students we have taught over the years who have posed interesting challenges and who in many ways have become teachers for us; the teachers we have met in staff rooms, workshops and seminars in many countries who have shared their insights and asked questions that became guidelines in our own search for excellence in teaching teenagers.

A number of authors whose writings have been important for us in giving shape to the thinking behind *English in Mind*: Kieran Egan, for his valuable insights into the psychology of the teenage student that have helped us enormously to find the right content for the books; Howard Gardner, Robert Dilts and Earl Stevick, for helping us understand more about the wonders of the human mind; Mihaly Csikszentmihalyi , for his insights into the flow state, without which our own work would have been much less enjoyable.

The team at Pentacor Book Design for giving the book its design; Anne Rosenfeld for the audio recordings; Meredith Levy, Hilary Ratcliff, Annie Cornford, Fran Banks and Ruth Pellegrini for their excellent editorial support; and all other people involved in creating this course.

Last, but not least we would like to thank our partners, Mares and Adriana, for their support.

The authors and publishers would like to thank the teachers who commented on the material at different stages of its development:

Belgium: Chantal Alexandrer; Marie-Christine Callaert; David Collie; Myriam Deplechin; Denise De Vleeschauwer; Claude Hallett; Valerie Hirsoux; Marie-Louise Leujeune Claes; Ingrid Quix; Cecile Rouffiange Donckers; Bruno Tremault; Edithe van Eycke; Patrick Verheyen; Jan Vermeiren. Italy: Elena Assirelli; Gloria Gaiba; Grazia Maria Niccolaioni; Deanna Serantoni Donatini; Cristiana Ziraldo. Poland: Malgorzata Dyszlewska; Ewa Paciorek; Julita Moninska; Pawel Morawski; Dorota Muszynska; Switzerland: Irena Engelmann; Niki Low; Susan Ann Sell.

We would also like to thank all the teachers who allowed us to observe their classes, and who gave up their valuable time for interviews and focus groups.

The publishers are grateful to Onward Music Ltd (Bucks Music Group) for permission to reproduce the lyrics to *Space Oddity* by David Bowie on page 93, and to Marathon Music International Limited, www.mmiuk.com, for the sound recording, © Marathon Music.

The publishers are grateful to the following for permission to reproduce photographic material:

Art Director's and Trip p. 14; Corbis pp. 5(5), 8, 12(tr), 12(b), 16(b), 23, 24, 28-29, 49(2), 49(4), 56(b); Eye Ubiquitous p. 14(m); Getty Images pp. 5(6), 7, 12(tl), 12(mr), 14(t), 16(t), 17(r) 20, 21, 32(2), 33(5), 34(tr), 40, 49(1), 49(3), 49(5), 56(l), 56-57(m), 57(r); Impact Photos pp. 5(4), 6; Rex Features pp. 33(3), 33(4), 52(a), 52(c); Topham pp. 5(3), 12(ml), 17(l); Zooid Pictures pp. 52(b), 52(e).

All other photographs taken by Gareth Boden.

The publishers are grateful to the following illustrators:

Dan Alexander, c/o Advocate Illustration p. 36; Kate Charlesworth p. 44; Yane Christensen, c/o Advocate Illustration pp. 35, 41; Mark Duffin pp. 18, 45, 60; Mandy Greatorex, c/o New Division p. 40; Sophie Joyce pp. 13, 26; Ken Oliver, c/o Wildlife Art p. 34; Peters & Zabransky pp. 6, 26; David Shenton pp. 11, 16, 25, 37, 48, 53, 55; Kim Smith, c/o Eastwing Illustration Agency p. 61; Kath Walker pp. 23, 25, 37, 48; Darrell Warner, c/o Beehive Illustration pp. 15, 27, 53; Stuart Williams, c/o The Organisation pp. 17, 29, 51.

The publishers are grateful to the following for their assistance with commissioned photographs: Parkside Community College, Cambridge; Christ's School, Richmond, London; The Jackie Palmer Agency.

The publishers are grateful to the following contributors:

Gareth Boden: commissioned photography
Meredith Levy: editorial work
Ruth Pellegrini: permissions research, wordlist compilation
Pentacorbig: text design and layouts
Hilary Ratcliff: editorial work
Anne Rosenfeld: audio recordings
Sally Smith: photographic direction, picture research
Tim Wharton: music and recording of the song on page 70

Herbert Puchta and Jeff Stranks with Meredith Levy

English in Mind

* Combo 1B · Workbook

CAMBRIDGE
UNIVERSITY PRESS

Contents

1 The languages we speak

1 Grammar

Comparative adjectives

a Read what Sarah says about her mother. Find 12 adjectives and <u>underline</u> them.

> My mother is studying Russian in her free time. She goes to a small class at our local college and she practises conversation with an old friend of hers, who is an excellent teacher. The Russian alphabet is different from ours, and that was strange at first. But Mum is good at languages and she's very determined. She's planning a big holiday in Russia and Finland soon, and I think that's a really exciting idea.

b Write the adjectives and their comparative forms in the table.

| ~~exciting~~ ~~good~~ ~~small~~ | quiet | big | lonely | difficult | bad |
| expensive | successful | cheap | noisy | far | relaxing | old |

-er	more ...	irregular
small – smaller	*exciting – more exciting*	*good – better*

c Compare the two cafés. Write sentences with some of the adjectives from Exercise 1b.

1 *Café Paradiso is smaller than Efes Café.*

2

3

4

5

6

Efes Café

30th birthday specials this week!!

- Our famous coffee – just $1.40

- A range of sandwiches at $4.50

Big games room with video screen and five pool tables

Café Paradiso

Just opened!!

Coffee $1.25

Fresh sandwiches from only $3.25

■   ■   ■   ■   ■

Small but friendly, relaxing atmosphere

---

2 Vocabulary

Language learning

a Match the words and phrases to make expressions about language learning.

1	have	a	the meaning of a word
2	imitate	b	in a dictionary
3	make	c	other speakers
4	guess	d	mistakes
5	look up a word	e	an accent
6	translate from	f	mistake
7	correct a	g	word means
8	know what a	h	your first language

b Fill in the spaces with verbs from Exercise 2a.

If you don't know what a word ¹_____, try to ²_____ the meaning, or ³_____ the word in your dictionary.

All foreign speakers ⁴_____ an accent, but that doesn't matter. To make your pronunciation better, listen to English speakers and try to ⁵_____ them. Don't worry if you ⁶_____ mistakes – that's normal!

It's often useful to ⁷_____ words from one language to the other, but it's best when you can start to think in the new language.

3 Grammar

Superlative adjectives

a Write the adjectives and their superlative forms.

~~high~~ ~~boring~~ beautiful bad big important easy good
thin delicious heavy creative short rich intelligent

-est	most ...	irregular
high – highest	boring – most boring	

b Complete the sentences. Use superlative adjectives from Exercise 3a.

1 All the food is nice here, but the fish soup is the _____ thing on the menu.

2 The size of London is about 1,580 km². It's one of the _____ cities in Europe.

3 That was the _____ lesson of the week! I nearly went to sleep.

4 Marilyn Monroe was one of the _____ women in Hollywood in the 1950s.

5 Maths is the _____ subject at school. I don't have any problems with it.

6 Mr Thomas has an amazing house near the beach and he owns four cars. He's the _____ person in our town.

7 This is the _____ bag in the world! What have you got in it?

Comparative or superlative?

(c) Read Sheila's email to her friend Simon in Sydney.
Write the correct forms in the spaces.

Hi Simon!

I'm writing this from London – we arrived here on
Tuesday, after staying in Madrid and Paris. London is
one of the ¹ _____ (interesting) cities in Europe,
but unfortunately it's also one of the ² _____
(expensive) places to stay. It's ³ _____ (big) than Paris and of course
it's a lot ⁴ _____ (old) than Sydney. You know I love history, and
there are lots of great museums here – in fact, I think the British Museum
is probably the ⁵ _____ (good) museum in the world. The people in
Madrid were ⁶ _____ (friendly) than London people, but it was
⁷ _____ (difficult) to communicate with them because I don't know
any Spanish. Paris was fantastic, of course, and I ate the ⁸ _____
(delicious) food of my life in some of the Paris restaurants.
My aunt, who's English, says that British food is ⁹ _____ (good) than
French, but she's wrong about that!

Tonight my aunt and uncle are taking me to a show: it's a musical called
The Phantom of the Opera. They say it's the ¹⁰ _____ (successful) show in
London. Of course I think it would be ¹¹ _____ (exciting) to see a pop concert,
but that would be the ¹² _____ (bad) thing in the world for my uncle and aunt.

We're flying home to Sydney in five days. See you then!

Sheila

(d) Write one comparative and one superlative sentence about the things in each group.
Use your own ideas.

Example

football – tennis – volleyball

Football is more exciting than tennis. Volleyball is the easiest sport.

1   New York – Rome – Rio de Janeiro

_____
_____
_____
_____

2   winter – spring – summer

_____
_____
_____
_____

3   rock music – rap music – classical music

_____
_____
_____
_____

4   English – French – Japanese

_____
_____
_____
_____

4 Pronunciation

Sentence stress

(a) 🔊 Listen and underline the syllables with the main stress.

1 Cars are faster than bicycles.
2 Chocolate is sweeter than butter.
3 Paula is more creative than her brother.
4 The Maths exam was more difficult than the Science one.
5 Robert is the youngest student in our class.
6 Vegetables are the healthiest things you can eat.
7 It was the most expensive jacket in the shop.
8 They were some of the most talented writers in the country.

(b) 🔊 Listen again and circle the syllables with the /ə/ sound. Then listen, check and repeat.

5 Everyday English

Underline the correct words.

1 I love your shirt. It's *crazy/cool/cruel*.
2 A: Let's watch *Teen Time* on television.
   B: You *must/can/can't* be serious! It's a really bad programme.
3 I don't want to spend all my *pocket/ rocket/packet* money. I have to *give/ shut/save* up to buy some new jeans.
4 A: I feel like getting a hamburger. *What about you? / So what? / What is it?*
   B: No, I want to *get out / check out / pick up* the new pizza place in West Street.

6 Study help

Self-assessment

Use these questions to help you to think about your progress as a language learner.

1 Why are you studying English? Give three reasons.

   ----

2 Are you better at English now than two months ago? What are some things you can do now that you couldn't do then?

   ----

3 What are some things that you want to talk about or understand in English?

   ----

4 Which area of English language learning is the easiest for you? Which is the most difficult? Put them in order from 1 (easiest) to 6 (most difficult).

   a understanding and remembering grammar ☐
   b learning vocabulary ☐
   c reading ☐
   d writing ☐
   e listening ☐
   f speaking ☐

5 How much time do you spend working on the area(s) you have problems with?

   ----

6 What ideas can you think of to help you improve?

Skills in mind

7 Listen

a Listen to Adrian talking about his sisters, Mary, Juliette, Carla and Alice. Match the people in the picture with their names and with the things they own.

Adrian   Mary   Juliette   Carla   Alice

b Listen again. Mark the statements *T* (true) or *F* (false).

1   Mary was born before the other girls. ☐
2   Adrian doesn't like Mary's hair. ☐
3   Juliette is an intelligent girl. ☐
4   Juliette is funnier than Mary. ☐
5   Carla and Alice often argue about animals. ☐
6   Carla is good at swimming. ☐

8 Write

Choose one of these topics:

- three members of your family
- three singers/groups
- three sports stars
- three TV/film stars who are popular in your country.

Write a paragraph to compare the three people you chose. Use comparative and superlative adjectives.

Listening tip

Here's an idea for practising your listening outside the classroom. Work with a friend. Every week, prepare a message in English and record it on a cassette. Exchange cassettes and listen to your friend's message. The topic of your message can be anything that interests you.

If you have a cassette recorder at home, you can start now – use Adrian's recording as an example and describe the people in your family.

Other ideas for listening practice outside the class:

- Listen to English speakers and try to hear what they are saying.

- Record programmes in English from the radio (for example, some of the BBC World Service programmes) and play them back.

- Watch films/videos in English with sub-titles. Cover the sub-titles as you watch and try to understand the dialogue.

- Listen to pop songs in English. If you want to read the words while you listen, you can probably find them on the Internet.

Unit check

1 Fill in the spaces

Complete the text with the words in the box.

> easier   guess   speak   ~~came~~   accent   worst   than   imitate   difficult   look

Michelle and Luc were born in France but their family _____came_____ to live in Verona two years ago, and now they both [1]_____ Italian. Michelle is older [2]_____ her brother and at first she found the new language more [3]_____ to learn. 'I think it's [4]_____ to pick up a language when you're younger,' she said. For her, pronunciation is the [5]_____ problem. 'A lot of Italian vocabulary is similar to French, so I can often [6]_____ the meaning of words – I don't have to [7]_____ them up in a dictionary,' she said. 'But I still have a strong French [8]_____ and sometimes people find it difficult to understand me. As soon as Luc went to school, he began to [9]_____ the other children, and he speaks almost perfect Italian now.'

9

2 Choose the correct answers

Circle the correct answers, a, b or c.

1 Jessie _____ four languages.
   a (speaks) b says c tells
2 I don't want to _____ any mistakes in my Maths test.
   a do b make c get
3 They're _____ a book from German into English.
   a correcting b translating c communicating
4 Look _____ these words in your dictionary.
   a up b down c to

5 Young children usually _____ their parents.
   a communicate b imitate c guess
6 He's one of the _____ film stars in the world.
   a most successful b successfuller
   c successfullest
7 Ruth was _____ than the other students in the class.
   a tall b taller c the tallest
8 Mrs Wilson is the _____ person in our street.
   a more friendly b friendliest c more friendliest
9 All the dishes were great, but the soup was _____ .
   a the better b the bettest c the best

8

3 Correct the mistakes

In each sentence there is a mistake with comparatives or superlatives.
Underline the mistake and write the correct sentence.

1 IT was the <u>easyest</u> subject at school last year. _IT was the easiest subject at school last year._
2 I think History is more interesting then Geography. _____
3 Mont Blanc is the higher mountain in Europe. _____
4 The book was more good than the film. _____
5 Your hamburger is biger than mine! _____
6 Football is the popularest sport in the world. _____
7 The Science exam was worst than the Maths exam. _____
8 My cat is most intelligent than my dog. _____
9 The day I met Laura was the more lucky day of my life. _____

8

How did you do?

Total: [25]

☺	Very good 20 – 25	☺	OK 14 – 19	☹	Review Unit 1 again 0 – 13

2 We're going on holiday

1 Remember and check

Think back to Kate's holiday plans and put the pictures in order. Write 1–5 in the boxes. Then check with the dialogue on page 13.

a

b

c

d

e

2 Grammar

Present continuous for future arrangements

a Complete the text about Kate's plans. Use the present continuous form of the verbs.

Kate ¹_____ (not stay) at home next August. She ²_____ (have) a holiday in Ireland with her family. Her parents ³_____ (pay) for the holiday and Kate's brother Greg ⁴_____ (go) too. They ⁵_____ (not fly) to Ireland – they ⁶_____ (travel) from England by ferry. Kate told me, 'I ⁷_____ (not hike) this year because Greg doesn't want to do that. But we ⁸_____ (spend) a week on a canal boat and we ⁹_____ (stay) on a farm on the Aran Islands. I'm really looking forward to it.'

b Alan wants to invite Marta to his house one afternoon next week – but which day? Look at Marta's diary and write her replies.

Mon
Helen coming to my place

Tues
Go shopping with Dad

Wed
Study for Maths test

Thurs
Tennis with Jane

Fri
4.30 Meet Uncle Jack at airport

Sat
Lunch with Grandma

Sun
Cousins arriving from Germany

1 **Thursday?** *Sorry, I'm playing tennis with Jane on Thursday.*

2 **Saturday?** _____

3 **Friday?** _____

4 **Sunday?** _____

5 **Monday?** _____

6 **Wednesday?** _____

7 **Tuesday?** _____

(c) Complete the dialogues with questions and short answers. Use the present continuous form of the verbs.

Martin: It's my birthday next Friday.

Caroline: That's nice. _Are you having_ (you / have) a party?

Martin: Yes, _I am_ . And I want you to come.

Caroline: Fantastic! Thanks, Martin. 1_____ (Peter / come)?

Martin: No, 2_____ . He's working on Friday.

Caroline: Oh, I see. 3_____ (Ann and Paul / come)?

Martin: Yes, 4_____ .

Caroline: Oh, good!

Phil: 5_____ (you and your family / go) on holiday this year?

Sandra: Yes, 6_____ . We're visiting my aunt in Greece in July.

Phil: Great! 7_____ (you / travel) by boat?

Sandra: No, 8_____ . We're going by plane.

Phil: 9_____ (your sister / go) with you?

Sandra: Yes, 10_____ .

Present continuous: now or in the future?

(d) Look at the underlined verbs. Are they about now or about the future? Write N (now) or F (future).

Jenny: Hello, it's Jenny speaking.

Enrico: Hi, Jenny. It's Enrico here. What <u>are</u> you <u>doing</u> (*N*)?

Jenny: Hi, Enrico. Oh, nothing much. We're having (¹____) dinner in a few minutes. What about you?

Enrico: Me? I'm watching (²____) the football on TV. It isn't a very good game.

Jenny: Yeah? Who's winning? (³____)

Enrico: France, 2–0. But listen, Jenny, what are you doing (⁴____) on Saturday?

Jenny: Saturday? I'm not doing (⁵____) anything. Why?

Enrico: Well, Adam and I are meeting (⁶____) at the beach. We want some more friends there. Do you want to come?

Jenny: Yes, OK.

Enrico: Great. We're having (⁷____) lunch there at about one o'clock.

Jenny: OK. My mum and I are doing (⁸____) some shopping in the morning. I can buy some food and bring it with me.

Enrico: Excellent!

Jenny: Look, I can't talk any more now – Dad's calling (⁹____) me. But I'll see you on Saturday, OK?

Enrico: OK, fine. See you then.

3 Vocabulary

Future time expressions

(a) Replace the underlined words with time expressions from the box.

> next week/month/year   the day after tomorrow
> the week/month/year after next
>
> in [number] { days'
>   weeks'
>   hours'   } time
>   months'
>   years' }

1 It's June now. The holidays are beginning in July.

   next month

2 Today is Wednesday. I'm going to the dentist on Friday.

   ....

3 It's four o'clock now. The programme starts at seven.

   ....

4 It's 2004 now. We're buying a new car in 2005.

   ....

5 It's February now. My brother is coming home in April.

   ....

6 It's Saturday 4th May today. Brian is playing basketball
   on Saturday 25th May.

   ....

Holiday activities

(b) Complete the crossword.

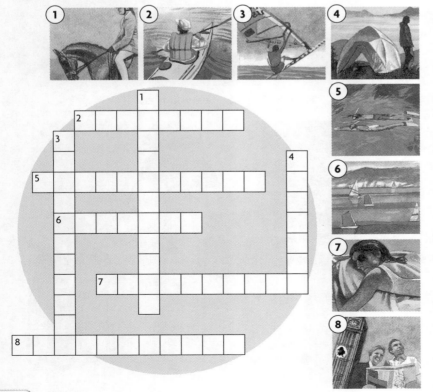

(c) Write the words in the lists to make expressions for talking about holiday activities.

> by plane   a boat   at home
> a week   souvenirs   a postcard
> on a farm   a car   some time
> to London   by car   three days
> presents   canoes   in a hotel

stay   *at home*
        ....
        ....

travel ....
        ....

hire   ....
        ....

spend   ....
        ....

buy   ....
        ....

(d) Complete the sentences with expressions from Exercise 3c.

1 I want to remember this place!
   I'd like to ....
   some ....

2 They were away for a week.
   They .... in
   Greece and four days in
   Germany.

3 We .... at the
   airport and drove round Ireland.

4 A: How did you get to Prague?
   B: I .... There
      was a flight at three o'clock.

5 A: Did you go camping in France?
   B: No, we ....
      in Paris.

4 Pronunciation

/θ/ (think) and /ð/ (that)

a 🔊 How do you say *th* in these words?
Write them in the correct lists.
Then listen, check and repeat.

clothes those Maths father thousand
thirteen athlete throw brother

/θ/ (th<u>in</u>k)	/ð/ (<u>th</u>at)

b 🔊 Listen and repeat.

1 It's my sixteenth birthday next month.
2 They're sunbathing together on the beach.
3 Her grandfather is healthy but he's very thin.
4 My brother can throw this ball further than me.

5 Culture in mind

Match the two parts of each word and write the words on the pictures.

1 back   cano
2 water   le
3 vol   pack
4 air   tle
5 tur   fall
6 jung   port

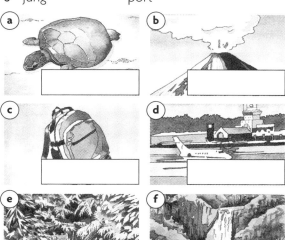

6 Study help

Using a dictionary

a Here are some abbreviations (short forms) that you find in a dictionary. Can you work out what the words are?

1 *n*   noun
2 *v*   ....
3 *adj*   ....
4 *prep*   ....
5 *sing*   ....
6 *pl*   ....

b Look at the dictionary entry for *cancel* and match the parts with the words in the box. Write the letters a–e.

1 ☐   2 ☐   3 ☐

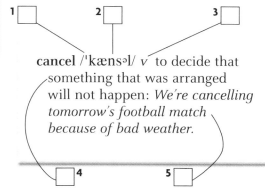

cancel /ˈkænsəl/ *v* to decide that something that was arranged will not happen: *We're cancelling tomorrow's football match because of bad weather.*

4 ☐   5 ☐

a the meaning of the word
b an example using the word
c the pronunciation
d the part of speech (noun, verb, etc.)
e the main stress

c Read the entry for *reservation*.

reservation /rezəˈveɪʃən/ *n* an arrangement for something like a seat on an aircraft or a table at a restaurant to be kept for you: *I'd like to make a table reservation for two people for 9 o'clock.*

Choose the correct meaning for this sentence: *We cancelled our hotel reservation.*

1 We now have a room at the hotel.
2 We no longer have a room at the hotel.
3 We couldn't get a room at the hotel.

Skills in mind

7 Read

Read Emma's email to Adam and answer the questions.

1 Who is 50 years old next week?

Emma's father

2 When and where are they having the party?

....

3 Who is coming from Greece?

....

4 When are they arriving?

....

5 Why aren't they staying at Emma's house?

....

6 Who can't come to the party? Why?

....

7 What are Emma and her mother doing tomorrow?

....

Hi Adam!

Guess what? Next week is my father's 50th birthday, and we're having a party on Saturday night. It's a secret – Dad doesn't know about it. My mum, my brother and I are organising it. We're using a big room in a hotel in town and we're bringing in flowers and putting up decorations on Saturday morning. We're hiring a jazz band to play music during the evening.

My aunt and uncle are coming from Greece. They're arriving on Friday, and they're staying in the hotel because our flat is very small. But my grandfather can't come because he's still in hospital. I'm very sad about that.

We're inviting all Dad's friends. Mum's making a birthday cake and she's hiring a catering company to serve food and drink. Tomorrow morning she and I are going out to buy some new clothes to wear. I hope I can find something nice!

I'll get in touch after the party and tell you all about it.

Love,

Emma

8 Listen

Listen to the phone conversation between Emma and Adam after the party. Were the party arrangements successful? Write ✓ if things were good and write ✗ if there was a problem.

Unit check

1 Fill in the spaces

Complete the text with the words in the box.

| aren't | is | breakfast | ~~holiday~~ | sunbathing | campsites | sailing | youth | coach | hiring |

Next month Richard and Kevin are having a ___holiday___ in Cornwall in the west of England. They're travelling by [1]_____ to the town of St Ives, and for the first four nights they're staying in a bed & [2]_____ on the coast. They like water sports, so they want to go [3]_____ and windsurfing, and they also plan to spend some time [4]_____ on the beach. After that, the boys are [5]_____ bikes to ride in the countryside. They [6]_____ taking much money with them, so they checked out cheap places to stay – usually they're staying at [7]_____ , but they're also spending a few nights in a [8]_____ hostel near Boscastle. They're coming back to London on 16th August and Richard's father [9]_____ meeting them at the bus station.

9

2 Choose the correct answers

Circle the correct answers, a, b or c.

1 Sandra went _____ on the river.
   a snorkelling   b canoeing   c horse-riding
2 You can hire _____ at the beach.
   a postcards   b hotels   c surfboards
3 We travelled from Italy to Greece _____ ferry.
   a on   b by   c with
4 Caroline and Ros are _____ three months in Africa.
   a spending   b saving   c camping

5 I need to buy a _____ for this letter.
   a souvenir   b stamp   c present
6 _____ working in the restaurant next weekend.
   a I not   b I'm not   c I don't
7 Where _____ for his next holiday?
   a he going   b he's going   c is he going
8 It's January now, so March is the month after _____ .
   a next   b today   c tomorrow
9 We're leaving for Australia in four months' _____ .
   a weekend   b time   c next

8

3 Correct the mistakes

In each sentence there is a mistake with the present continuous or with future time expressions. Underline the mistake and write the correct sentence.

1 <u>We visit</u> our aunt next Tuesday. _We're visiting our aunt next Tuesday._

2 My friend is arriving the day after the next. _____

3 Are you cook the dinner this evening? _____

4 My brother not going out this weekend. _____

5 Helen and Tony bring some CDs to the party on Friday. _____

6 I'm starting a new job the day next tomorrow. _____

7 Rebecca doesn't sing at the concert next week. _____

8 Stefano is seeing the doctor for three days' time. _____

9 When Alex is coming home from school this afternoon? _____

8

How did you do?

Total: **25**

| ☺ | Very good 20 – 25 | ☺ | OK 14 – 19 | ☹ | Review Unit 2 again 0 – 13 |

③ What will happen?

1 Grammar

will/won't

(a) 🔊 Read these parts of the dialogue from page 18. Fill in the spaces with the words in the box. Then listen and check.

> it'll be   they'll break you
> we'll all be   I'll never forget
> Will we find   it won't hurt

Samantha: Jake, we went into space nearly two years ago and we're still looking for planet Vulcan. What do you think?

¹_____ it?

Jake: Oh, yeah. I'm sure we will.

Jake: You have to do something!

Computer: Sorry! I'd like to help, but the spaceship is out of control and there's nothing – I repeat, nothing – I can do. So in 45 seconds, ²_____ _____ dead.

Samantha: Help! Do something!

Computer: I can't. But don't worry. When we die, in exactly ... 30 seconds from now, ³_____ _____ very quick and

⁴_____ !

Computer: Five seconds!

Jake: ⁵_____ you, Sam.

Computer: April Fool!

Samantha: Oh! When we get back to Earth, I'm going to tell them about you, and ⁶_____ _____ into little pieces.

(b) Match the sentences with the pictures. Write the numbers 1–8 in the boxes.

1 Jim, come on! Quickly! We _____ late for school!

2 Don't worry about tomorrow's test. I'm sure it _____ very difficult.

3 They _____ today. There aren't any good players in the team.

4 I don't know how to fix this! I'll call Bob – I'm sure he _____ me.

5 Let's look on the Internet. Perhaps we _____ some information there.

6 Please don't buy that dress for me, Mum. I _____ it.

7 Don't be scared. The dog _____ us.

8 Please sit down. The doctor _____ you soon.

(c) Complete the sentences in Exercise 1b. Use *will* or *won't* with the verbs in the box.

> help   be   find   see   not be   not hurt
> not wear   not win

d Read the answers and complete the questions.

1 A: .... Liz and Graham .... married?

   B: Yes, I think they will. They really love each other.

2 A: What do you think? .... Clare .... to the party?

   B: Yes, of course she'll come.

3 A: .... Jenny .... to university when she leaves school?

   B: No, she won't. She wants to go to art school.

4 A: It's late! .... your parents .... angry?

   B: Well, they won't be very happy.

5 A: When .... Chris .... painting his room?

   B: I think he'll finish it tomorrow.

6 A: Where .... you .... Alan?

   B: I'll see him at the sports club on Friday.

e Matt is visiting a fortune teller. The pictures show what she sees in her crystal ball. Write her predictions for Matt's future.

1 _You'll go to university_ and _you'll become a vet_ .

2 .... , but ....

3 .... , but ....

4 .... , but ....

f Complete the sentences with your own predictions. Use 'll/will or won't.

1 In a few years' time, I ....

2 When I leave school, I ....

3 Before I'm 30, I ....

4 I think my best friend ....

5 In the future, my town ....

6 In 20 years' time, ...

2 Pronunciation

will, 'll or nothing?

a 🔊 Listen and repeat.

I'll go now.
She'll help you.
They'll be here on Monday.
You'll see him later.
That information will be on the Internet.
The universe will continue to get bigger.

b 🔊 Listen and write what you hear: *will, 'll* or *0* (nothing). Then listen again and check.

1 Don't worry. I _____ do this for you.

2 We _____ do our homework after lunch.

3 The spaceship _____ land in 20 minutes.

4 The countdown _____ start soon.

5 During a flight, astronauts _____ eat lots of vitamins.

6 Go to university. I'm sure you _____ see how important it is for your future.

7 I doubt they _____ be here in half an hour.

8 They say this capsule _____ take people to the planet Jupiter.

3 Vocabulary

Expressions to talk about the future

a Make sentences from the box for each situation below.

I think I don't think	he'll give it back. he'll know how to do it. the baby will wake up. they'll be late. I'll finish before 9 o'clock. I'll enjoy it.

1 I want to watch this film.
_____

2 Please don't talk so loudly.
_____

3 Don't give your CD player to Tom.
_____

4 This exercise is hard! Let's talk to Sam.
_____

5 My friends will be here soon.
_____

6 I'm still doing my homework.
_____

b Complete the sentences with the words in the box.

doubt	hope	probably	maybe	sure	not sure

1 Catherine _____ won't pass her test. She hasn't done much work.

2 I _____ Jules will go to the concert. He doesn't enjoy pop music.

3 I sent the letter yesterday, but I'm _____ when it will arrive.

4 We don't know what we're doing in the summer, but _____ we'll go to Turkey.

5 Tessa and John _____ to get married next year.

6 I bought a lovely scarf for Annie. I'm _____ she'll like it.

c Fill in the puzzle. The answers are all in the song on page 21.

① S
② P
③ _ _ A
④ _ C
⑤ _ E

4 Everyday English

Complete the dialogue with expressions from page 23.

Bill: So, what would you like, Jenny?

Jenny: Oh, a cappuccino, please.

Bill: ¹_____ _____ ?
Something to eat?

Jenny: No, thanks.

Waitress: Are you ready to order?

Bill: Just two cappuccinos, please.

(The waitress brings the cappuccinos.)

Bill: Jenny, what are you doing?

Jenny: I'm trying to put the sugar into the cappuccino – but I want to keep the chocolate on the top! This is ² _____ _____ _____ about having a cappuccino.

Bill: Oh, Jenny! That's ³ _____ !

Jenny: Whoops! Oh, no!

Bill: Oh, I ⁴ _____ _____ it. There's sugar all over the table. How ⁵ _____ !

5 Study help

Using a dictionary

a You can often use the same word as different parts of speech. For example, the word *joke* can be a noun or a verb. The dictionary shows this difference.

> **joke** /dʒəʊk/ *n* a funny story or trick to make people laugh: *Did I tell you the joke about the chicken crossing the road?* • a person or thing that is ridiculous or not nearly good enough: *Let's go home – this football match is a joke.*
>
> *v* to say funny things: *They joked and laughed as they looked at the photos.*

Which sentence uses *joke* as a verb? Which sentences use it as a noun?

1 No one can understand the instructions on this box. They're a **joke**!
2 Don't **joke** about this – it isn't funny.
3 I heard a very good **joke** on the radio yesterday.

b You can also see that a word often has more than one meaning. Sometimes the meanings are similar (for example, the noun definitions 1 and 2 for *joke*), but sometimes they are quite different.

Read the dictionary entry for *land*. Then match the definitions with the sentences. Write a–d in the boxes.

> ⓐ
> ⓑ **land** /lænd/ *n.* the surface of the Earth that is not covered by water: *It is cheaper to drill for oil on land than at sea.* • an area in the countryside: *He has some land in the mountains. This land is good for fruit growing.*
> ⓒ *v.* to arrive at a place after moving down through the air: *I always feel nervous when the plane is landing.* • to bring an aircraft down to the Earth's surface: *You can land a plane on water in an emergency.*
> ⓓ

1 They grow wonderful tomatoes on their **land** in Tuscany. ☐
2 You can't **land** a helicopter in the middle of the forest! ☐
3 Hundreds of planes **land** at this airport every week. ☐
4 They couldn't see the **land** from the ship. ☐

Skills in mind

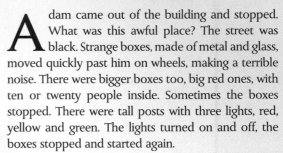

6 Read

This is part of a story about a man called Adam. In 1704 he went to sleep in London – but when he woke up, it was 300 years later.

Read the story. Find the parts where Adam sees these things:

1 a CD shop   _lines 18–21_

2 buses   _____

3 a policeman   _____

4 a police car   _____

5 a TV shop   _____

6 cars   _____

7 a clothes shop   _____

8 traffic lights   _____

7 Write

After he ran away from the policeman, Adam went into a cinema. Write the next paragraph of the story. Begin like this:

> Adam ran through some big doors.
> A woman shouted, 'Hey, you have to buy a ticket!' But Adam didn't stop.
> He pushed through a door and ...

Writing tip

Notice the way the text uses adjectives to create a clear picture and to show Adam's feelings. Underline all the adjectives in the first paragraph of the text. Then read the sentences without the adjectives and see how the picture loses life and colour.

- Use adjectives in your paragraph for Exercise 7. You can choose some from the box or use others that you know.

dark	dangerous	strange
loud	frightening	huge	angry
afraid	nervous	

Adam came out of the building and stopped. What was this awful place? The street was black. Strange boxes, made of metal and glass, moved quickly past him on wheels, making a terrible noise. There were bigger boxes too, big red ones, with ten or twenty people inside. Sometimes the boxes stopped. There were tall posts with three lights, red, yellow and green. The lights turned on and off, the boxes stopped and started again. 5

All around him, there were incredibly tall buildings. And the people! People everywhere. Many of them stopped and looked at him, then they turned and walked away quickly. Someone shouted to him: 'Hey, you! Are you lost? The theatre's over there!' and then laughed. Adam walked past windows, big glass windows with women inside, but the women didn't move. 10 15

At the next window, he heard loud noises coming out through an open door, and inside there were people looking at little square boxes – hundreds of little square boxes, all with different pictures. 20

Then another window, and here he saw larger boxes, this time with small people and houses inside them! Adam stopped again and looked around. One of the metal boxes in the street was near him – a black and white box with a blue light on top. A man in blue clothes and a strange hat got out and walked towards him. 'Excuse me, sir,' said the man. Adam didn't like him. He turned and ran. 25

—— 27 ——

Unit check

1 Fill in the spaces

Complete the text with the words in the box.

| probably | ~~won't~~ | nonsense | don't | she'll | to find | abroad | maybe | think | sure |

I know I ___won't___ get great results in my final exams, but I ¹_____ they'll be good enough for me to get into university. But before I start my university studies, I'd like to go ²_____ for a year. My friend Suzanne and I will ³_____ travel together in Asia and South America. When we come back, I think I'll study Environmental Science. I hope ⁴_____ an interesting job at the end of my course, but I ⁵_____ think I'll be rich or famous! Suzanne isn't ⁶_____ what she'll do in the future. She says she'll never be very successful, but that's ⁷_____ ! She's good at languages, so ⁸_____ she'll become a translator or a language teacher – who knows? I'm sure ⁹_____ have lots of success in her life, because she's a very intelligent person.

[ ] 9

2 Choose the correct answers

Circle the correct answers, a, b or c.

1 Earth is a _____ and it travels round the sun.
   a spaceship   b (planet)   c galaxy

2 A: Oh, no! I think I left my money at home.
   B: I don't _____ it! You can't be serious!
   a think   b know   c believe

3 A: Would you like anything _____ ?
   B: No, thank you. Just the bill, please.
   a else   b also   c after

4 My sister and her boyfriend are _____ married next month.
   a having   b doing   c getting

5 He has to work late, so he _____ won't come to the disco.
   a maybe   b probably   c doubts

6 It's a lovely morning. _____ it'll rain today.
   a I think   b I don't think   c I'm sure

7 They _____ to go to Cambridge University next year.
   a hope   b think   c doubt

8 Steve got bad results in the exam. His parents _____ be happy about that.
   a won't   b don't   c aren't

9 _____ find the information on the Internet?
   a We'll   b Do we will   c Will we

[ ] 8

3 Correct the mistakes

In each sentence there is a mistake with *will/won't* or with expressions to talk about the future. Underline the mistake and write the correct sentence.

1 Pietro won't <u>to live</u> abroad. *Pietro won't live abroad.* _____

2 This town is bigger in ten years' time. _____

3 Maybe they have guitar lessons next year. _____

4 I'll be sure Emma will get a good job. _____

5 You will watch a video this evening? _____

6 Lisa won't probably arrive before 10 o'clock. _____

7 Will your parents to drive us to the airport? _____

8 They doesn't go there again next year. _____

9 I won't think our team will win the competition. _____

[ ] 8

How did you do?

Total: [ ] 25

| ☺ Very good 20 – 25 | ☺ OK 14 – 19 | ☹ Review Unit 3 again 0 – 13 |

4 Never give up!

1 Remember and check

The pictures show events from the text on page 24. Put them in the correct order. Then check with the text.

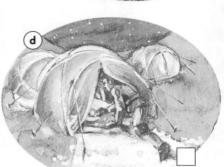

2 Grammar

too + adjective

a Match the sentences.

1 You won't get it all in that bag. a It's too long.
2 I won't finish this book tonight. b I get too nervous.
3 I need to lose some weight. c It's too loud.
4 We can't swim here. d It's too small.
5 I can't sleep before an exam. e I'm too fat.
6 Please turn the music down. f The water is too polluted.

b <u>Underline</u> the correct word, *very* or *too*.

1 They're *very / too* old.

2 No, you can't play. You're *very / too* old.

3 Wow! This is *very / too* heavy!

4 Oh, no! It's *very / too* heavy.

5 I think she's got a lot of money. Her car is *very / too* expensive.

6 It's *very / too* expensive for me. I've only got £10.

(c) Alex is talking to Amy – but he's saying some crazy things! Complete Amy's replies. Use an adjective from the box with *too*.

| cold | easy | expensive | far | difficult |
| small | ~~old~~ | young | | |

1 **Alex:** It's my grandmother's 80th birthday tomorrow. I'm taking her to a disco.

   Amy: You can't do that! She's _too old_ .

2 **Alex:** I think I can learn to speak Chinese and Russian in six months.

   Amy: No way! They're _____ _____ .

3 **Alex:** I'm going camping in Antarctica.

   Amy: You're joking! It's _____ _____ .

4 **Alex:** I'm going for a ride on my little brother's bike.

   Amy: You can't do that! It's _____ _____ for you.

5 **Alex:** My father wants to drive across Canada in two days.

   Amy: That's impossible. It's _____ _____ .

6 **Alex:** Tomorrow I'm taking my six-year-old sister to a Dracula film.

   Amy: You can't do that. She's _____ _____ .

7 **Alex:** Look at this test! One of the questions is: 2 + 2 = ?

   Amy: I don't believe you! That question's _____ .

8 **Alex:** On Saturday I'm buying some new shoes. They're €250.

   Amy: €250? Oh Alex, don't buy them. They're _____ .

3 Vocabulary
The weather

(a) Complete the sentences with adjectives to describe the weather.

1 It's _cool_ and _cloudy_ .

2 It's _____ and _____ .

3 Yesterday it was _____ and _____ .

4 They say it will be _____ and _____ tomorrow.

5 On 1st January it was _____ and _____ .

6 Today it's _____ and _____ .

(b) Answer the questions. Write full sentences.

1 What's the weather like today?

_____ .

2 What was the weather like last weekend?

_____ .

3 What do you think it will be like tomorrow?

_____ .

4 What's the weather like in your country in May?

_____ .

5 What's it like in November?

_____ .

4 Grammar

Adverbs

a Complete the table.

b Underline the correct words.

1 Work *quiet / quietly*, please. You're making too much noise.

2 I thought it was a *stupid / stupidly* film, so I stopped watching it.

3 They walked *slow / slowly* across the park.

4 I won't go in Jack's car. He drives too *dangerous / dangerously*.

5 My *usual / usually* breakfast is tea and toast.

6 You need to exercise if you want to be *healthy / healthily*.

Adjectives	Adverbs
quick	1 ....
safe	2 ....
3	noisily
4	early
hard	5 ....
brilliant	6 ....
7	well
8	fast
easy	9 ....
late	10 ....

c What are they doing? Write sentences about the people in the pictures. Use a verb from box A and an adverb from the adjectives in box B.

A

shout   work   play
win   ~~travel~~   smile
get up   run

B

quick   happy   loud
hard   bad   late
easy   ~~slow~~

   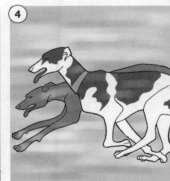

1 They *'re travelling slowly* .

2 She ....

3 He ....

4 The dogs ....

5 She ....

6 They ....

7 She ....

8 He ....

5 Culture in mind

Match the two parts of the words and then match the words with the definitions.

1	new	way	a	flats for people to live in
2	sky	ury	b	the verb from *success*
3	manu	ments	c	using your hands
4	rail	rants	d	people who arrived for the first time a short time ago
5	cent	eed	e	very tall buildings
6	mig	al	f	the train system
7	apart	comers	g	people who moved to a new country to live
8	succ	scrapers	h	100 years

6 Pronunciation

/ɒ/ and /əʊ/

a 🔊 Listen and repeat. Try to hear the difference between the /ɒ/ and the /əʊ/ sounds.

/ɒ/ job what want <u>fo</u>ggy be<u>lo</u>ng <u>pro</u>bably

/əʊ/ rope won't joke kil<u>o</u> <u>go</u>ing tomor<u>row</u>

b 🔊 <u>Underline</u> the words or syllables with the /ɒ/ sound. Circle the words or syllables with the /əʊ/ sound. Then listen again, check and repeat.

1 Our dog has got a cold nose.
2 Bob and Tom don't go to the coast.
3 The foreign politician told a good joke.
4 John wants to own a mobile phone.
5 Those tomatoes are old.
   So what? Throw them in the pot!

7 Study help

Spelling and pronunciation

It's often difficult to work out the spelling of English words from their sound, or to be sure how to pronounce them from their spelling. But there are some patterns that you can follow. Here are some common spellings for the /əʊ/ sound.

o	ow	oa	o + consonant + e
go	throw	coat	phone
....	....	....	....
....	....	....	....
....	....	....	....
....	....	....	....

Work out what these words are and add them to the lists:

/baʊt/ /tə'mɒrəʊ/ /pə'teɪtəʊ/ /nəʊz/ /dʒəʊk/
/'wɪndəʊ/ /hel'əʊ/ /səʊp/ /həʊp/ /'fɒləʊ/

You can build up similar spelling lists for other sounds. For example, here are some common spellings for the /ɜː/ sound. Can you add more words to the lists?

er	ur	ir
verb	turn	bird
....	....	....
....	....	....

- If you make lists like this, look at them regularly.
- Record difficult words on a cassette. Then test yourself by playing them and writing them down.

Skills in mind

8 Read

Read the questionnaire and choose the answers which are true for you. Then add up your score. Do you think the description is true about you?

9 Write

Choose one of the situations in the questionnaire and make it into a story. Write what happened.

Writing tip
Planning a narrative

● Plan the events in your story before you start to write. Use these questions to organise your ideas, and make notes for each question.

  1 Setting the scene: where and when did the events happen?

  2 What situation did you face?

  3 What did you do first?

  4 What happened after that?

  5 How did it end?

● When you are sure of the basic events, add some details to your plan. Try to 'see' the situation as clearly as you can. What did things/people look like? How did people behave? How did you feel? Quickly write down words and phrases that you can use.

● Now use your notes to start writing your story. Write a paragraph for each section (1–5). Don't forget:

  – use of connectors *and*, *but* and *because* to link ideas

  – use of adjectives and adverbs to give your story interest and colour.

How easily do you give up

① You have some very difficult homework to do. Do you …

  a give up? ○

  b keep working at it? ○

  c go away and do something else, then come back to the problem? ○

② You lend some money to a friend, but he/she doesn't give it back. Do you …

  a stop talking to your friend? ○

  b forget about the money? ○

  c ask your friend (nicely) to give you the money as soon as possible? ○

③ You see some clothes you really like, but they're very expensive. Do you …

  a feel angry and try to forget the clothes? ○

  b buy something cheaper? ○

  c start saving money to buy the clothes that you really want? ○

④ You know a boy/girl, and want to go out with him/her. But you know that he/she goes out with lots of other people. Do you …

  a forget about this person? ○

  b look for someone else to go out with? ○

  c ask him/her to go out with you and then see what happens? ○

⑤ You want to play for the school team in your favourite sport, but the teacher never chooses you. Do you …

  a decide not to do sport any more? ○

  b choose a different sport and try to get into that team? ○

  c practise harder and ask the teacher why he/she doesn't choose you? ○

For each *a* answer, give yourself 0 points.
For each *b* answer, give yourself 1 point.
For each *c* answer, give yourself 2 points.
Check your score.

8–10 points: Good for you! You don't give up easily.

4–7 points: Try a little harder to get the things you want.

0–3 points: Come on! If you don't try, you'll never get what you want.

Unit check

1 Fill in the spaces

Complete the text with the words in the box.

| happily   snowed   windy   angry   weather   too   ~~rainy~~   sunny   bitterly   heavily |

Usually the English winter is cold and ___rainy___, so my family decided to have a weekend break in the south of France last February. We wanted to enjoy some good weather. But when our plane landed at Nice, it was [1]_____ foggy to see anything through the windows, and before we got to our hotel it started to rain [2]_____ . On Saturday the weather was worse – it was [3]_____ and [4]_____ cold. And on Sunday it [5]_____ in Nice for the first time in 15 years! When we arrived back in England that evening, my uncle met us at the airport. 'The [6]_____ was fantastic here this weekend,' he said [7]_____ . 'It was beautifully warm and [8]_____ every day! How was Nice?' My father was too [9]_____ to answer him.

| 9 |

2 Choose the correct answers

Circle the correct answers, a, b or c.

1 It was terribly hot this afternoon, but it's nice and _____ now.
   a cool   b cold   c snowy

2 You have to drive slowly when it's _____ .
   a sunny   b warm   c foggy

3 We didn't see the sun today because it was too _____ .
   a windy   b cloudy   c hot

4 Don't forget your umbrella. They say it will _____ this afternoon.
   a rain   b rains   c raining

5 You can't learn to drive now. You're _____ young.
   a too   b much   c very

6 They came _____ into the room.
   a quiet   b quietly   c too quietly

7 I can do this work _____ .
   a easy   b easly   c easily

8 We were in the airport for an hour because the plane arrived _____ .
   a late   b lately   c later

9 I'm really happy. This result is _____ .
   a very good   b too good   c very well

| 8 |

3 Correct the mistakes

In each sentence there is a mistake with *too* + adjective or with adverbs.
Underline the mistake and write the correct sentence.

1 Drive <u>slow</u> – this bridge is dangerous. *Drive slowly – this bridge is dangerous.*

2 That music is very loudly. _____

3 The shop was busy and we had to work hardly. _____

4 It's to hot to wear a jumper. _____

5 If you walk quick, you can get to the station in five minutes. _____

6 My grandfather is too old, but he's fit and healthy. _____

7 Alison talks slow, so it's easy to understand her. _____

8 I can't lift the piano – it's too heavily. _____

9 Our team didn't win, but they played good. _____

| 8 |

How did you do?

Total: | 25 |

| ☺ | Very good 20 – 25 | ☺ | OK 14 – 19 | ☹ | Review Unit 4 again 0 – 13 |

5 Good intentions

1 Remember and check

Use the summary to fill in the puzzle. Check with the text on page 34.

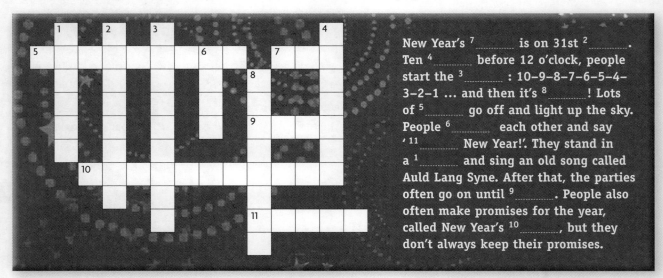

New Year's ⁷_____ is on 31st ²_____. Ten ⁴_____ before 12 o'clock, people start the ³_____: 10–9–8–7–6–5–4–3–2–1 ... and then it's ⁸_____! Lots of ⁵_____ go off and light up the sky. People ⁶_____ each other and say '¹¹_____ New Year!'. They stand in a ¹_____ and sing an old song called Auld Lang Syne. After that, the parties often go on until ⁹_____. People also often make promises for the year, called New Year's ¹⁰_____, but they don't always keep their promises.

2 Vocabulary

Phrasal verbs

a Match the two parts of the sentences.

1 I want to take up skiing,	a when I bought a new one.
2 I gave up smoking	b but I couldn't find the answer.
3 I tried to work out the problem,	c because I hated practising.
4 I threw away my old jumper	d because it was bad for my health.
5 I didn't keep up my piano lessons	e so I'll have to buy some warm clothes.

b Fill in the phrasal verbs. Use a word from each box.

work   throw   keep   give   take   up   out   away

1 They're playing brilliantly! I hope they can _____ it _____ .

2 Hey, don't _____ _____ those boxes! I'm going to use them.

3 I need some exercise. I think I'll _____ _____ a new sport.

Lesley, I think you'll have to _____ _____ skateboarding.

4 Can you _____ _____ where we are?

Write your own answers to the questions. What are ...

1 two things you should give up if you want to lose weight?

....

2 two things you will never throw away?

....

3 two activities you should keep up if you want to learn English well?

....

4 two activities you would like to take up when you're older?

....

3 Grammar

be going to: intentions

a Steve is getting ready to leave for a holiday. Look at the picture and mark the sentences *T* (true) or *F* (false).

1 Steve is going to have a holiday in Portugal. ☐
2 He's going to take his computer with him. ☐
3 He isn't going to drive to Barcelona. ☐
4 He's going to go snorkelling. ☐
5 He's going to stay at a campsite. ☐
6 He isn't going to take any photos. ☐

b Complete the sentences with the correct form of *be* (positive or negative).

1 I .... going to get up early tomorrow. I have to finish my French homework before school.

2 Greg .... going to meet his sister at the station. She's arriving at 9.30.

3 .... you going to watch the James Bond film on TV tonight?

4 We haven't got much money, so we .... going to stay in an expensive hotel.

5 Jane .... going to see the doctor because she's feeling much better now.

6 They've got some sandwiches, cake and fruit juice. They .... going to have lunch on the beach.

7 I .... going to catch the bus this afternoon. I want to walk home.

8 .... your cousin going to come to the New Year's Eve party?

c Complete the questions with the correct form of *be going to*. Then complete the short answers.

1 A: *Are* your brothers *going to fly* (fly) to Frankfurt?

B: No, *they aren't* .

2 A: .... Maria .... (learn) to drive?

B: Yes, ...

3 A: .... Andrew .... (move) to a new flat?

B: No, ...

4 A: .... you .... (wear) your red shirt tonight?

B: No, ...

5 A: .... Tim and Diane .... (do) the washing-up?

B: Yes, ...

6 A: .... we .... (hire) a houseboat?

B: Yes, ...

be going to: predictions

d Complete the sentences. Use the correct form of *be going to* with the verbs in the box.

miss   have   ~~not snow~~   not enjoy   not see

1 It *isn't going to snow* _____ again this afternoon.

2 I _____ this film.

3 They _____ an argument.

4 We _____ anything up there.

5 You _____ the train!

e What's going to happen? Write sentences with *be going to*. Use your own ideas.

1 Come on! Your dinner is on the table.

   It's going to get cold. _____

2 Ruth didn't get a good result in her exam.

   _____

3 No one can beat the Italian cyclists.

   _____

4 The car is out of control!

   _____

5 Stop climbing on that rope!

   _____

6 Patrick ate two hamburgers and some chocolate for lunch.

   _____

must / mustn't

f Complete the school rules. Use *must* and *mustn't* and a verb from the box.

wear   use   be   do   bring   eat

BISHOPWOOD GIRLS' SCHOOL

School rules

1   You _____ food during classes.

2   You _____ your homework.

3   You _____ your mobile phone in the classroom.

4   Every student _____ a school uniform.

5   Students _____ pets to school.

6   Students _____ quiet when they are in the library.

4 Pronunciation

must/mustn't

🔊 Listen and <u>underline</u> the words you hear. Then listen again and repeat.

1 You *must/mustn't* do that.
2 You *must/mustn't* sit here.
3 She *must/mustn't* speak to him.
4 We *must/mustn't* give her the letter.
5 I *must/mustn't* stay here.
6 You *must/mustn't* forget me.

5 Everyday English

Making offers

Complete the dialogues. Use a phrase from each box.

I'll drive	it for you.
I'll open	an omelette for you.
I'll ask	for your meal.
I'll pay	you home.
I'll fix	my parents.
I'll make	the window.

1 A: I've missed the bus!
   B: That's OK. ....

2 A: My CD player isn't working.
   B: Don't worry. ....

3 A: I haven't got any money with me.
   B: That's all right. ....

4 A: It's hot in here.
   B: ....

5 A: I'd like something to eat.
   B: OK. ....

6 A: Can we have the party at your place?
   B: I don't know. ....

6 Study help

Speaking

Here's an idea to help you practise speaking English outside the classroom. Record a list of questions about your activities and interests. Later, play back the questions and answer them aloud. Do this once or twice a week – your answers will be different at different times. After a few weeks, add more questions or record new ones.

If you have a cassette recorder at home, you can start now. Record these questions and add two more of your own.

Where are you at the moment?
Did you have a good day at school today?
What was the weather like?
Who did you have lunch with?
Did you see [*someone's name*] after school?
When did you get home?
What did you have for dinner last night?
Did you watch anything interesting on television yesterday?
What did you do last weekend?
What are you going to do tomorrow?

....

....

....

....

Other ideas for speaking practice:

● Practise dialogues with a friend – help each other with expression and pronunciation when you can. If possible, record your dialogues, listen together and then practise again.

● Try to talk in English for 15–20 minutes every day with a friend. Perhaps you can do this when you are coming to school or going home.

● Leave a voice message in English on your friend's phone. When you get a message from your friend, ring back to leave a reply.

● If you know any English speakers, have conversations with them as often as you can.

Skills in mind

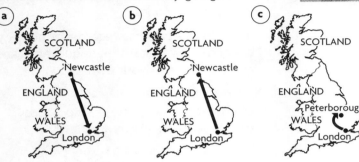

7 Listen

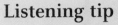 It's 1st January and Denise is ringing Robbie, a friend in America. Listen to the dialogue and (circle) the correct answers, a, b or c.

1 Where are Denise and her family going?

ⓐ
SCOTLAND
Newcastle
ENGLAND
WALES
London

ⓑ
SCOTLAND
Newcastle
ENGLAND
WALES
London

ⓒ
SCOTLAND
ENGLAND
Peterborough
WALES
London

2 When are they going to move?

ⓐ next weekend   ⓑ in five weeks' time   ⓒ in nine weeks' time

3 Which is their new house?

ⓐ FOR SALE SOLD — 4 bedrooms, garden
ⓑ FOR SALE SOLD — 3 bedrooms, garden
ⓒ FOR SALE SOLD — 2 bedrooms, garden

4 How does Denise feel about selling the flat?

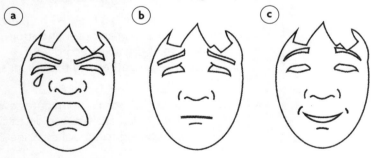

ⓐ   ⓑ   ⓒ

5 What is Denise's mother going to do?

 ⓐ
 ⓑ
 ⓒ

Listening tip

Using tapescripts

For extra practice with this listening text, you can ask your teacher to give you the tapescript.

- Use the tapescript to listen and read at the same time. Pause after each person's speech and read it aloud.

- Use white corrector fluid to 'white out' parts of the text – for example, you could remove all the verbs, or you could remove every sixth word. Perhaps your teacher will do this for you, or you could do it for a partner and then exchange tapescripts. A day or two later, listen to the recording again and try to fill in all the spaces.

8 Write

Imagine that you are Denise. Write an email to a different friend. Tell her about the things you and your family are going to do this year.

Unit check

1 Fill in the spaces

Complete the text with the words in the box.

| going   to   take   resolutions   keep   ~~Year's~~   give   isn't   must   stick |

Now that it's New ___Year's___ Day, everyone is making [1]_____ for the year. I'd like to get into the school basketball team this year, and that means I really [2]_____ get fitter. So I'm [3]_____ to start running in the mornings before school. It [4]_____ going to be easy. I tried it once or twice last year, but I found it boring on my own and I didn't [5]_____ it up. But this time Bruno is going [6]_____ come running with me, and I think this will help me to [7]_____ to my resolution. Bruno is determined to lose some weight, so he says he's going to [8]_____ up hamburgers and chocolate, and he's also going to [9]_____ up gymnastics. This is going to be the year of healthy living!

[ ] 9

2 Choose the correct answers

Circle the correct answers, a, b or c.

1 You must try to _____ up smoking.
   a take   b keep   c (give)

2 I'm going to throw _____ these old shoes.
   a away   b up   c down

3 It's a difficult question. Can you _____ the answer?
   a work out   b take up   c put on

4 You're cold! I'll _____ you a jumper.
   a giving   b going to give   c give

5 It's getting late. _____ leave soon.
   a We must   b Must we   c We mustn't

6 Julio _____ going to meet us at the airport.
   a will   b is   c are

7 You _____ drive too fast.
   a must   b mustn't   c going to

8 _____ Julia going to sing with the band?
   a Does   b Will   c Is

9 A: I can't lift this box. B: _____ you.
   a I help   b I'll help   c I'm helping

[ ] 8

3 Correct the mistakes

In each sentence there is a mistake with *be going to* or with *must/mustn't*.
Underline the mistake and write the correct sentence.

1 I'm going <u>clean</u> my room this weekend. *I'm going to clean my room this weekend.*

2 We going to study hard before the exams. _____

3 Anna doesn't go to watch TV this evening. _____

4 They must being home before 12 o'clock. _____

5 I not going to take my guitar with me. _____

6 You going to take up windsurfing next year? _____

7 We mustn't to forget Mum's birthday. _____

8 Does it going to rain soon? _____

9 They don't going to travel by bus. _____

[ ] 8

How did you do?

Total: 25

| ☺ Very good 20 – 25 | ☺ OK 14 – 19 | ☹ Review Unit 5 again 0 – 13 |

6 You shouldn't do that!

1 Grammar

should/shouldn't

a Match the pictures with the sentences in the text. Write the numbers 1–4 in the boxes. Then complete the sentences with *should* or *shouldn't*.

b Complete the sentences. Use the phrases in the box with should or shouldn't.

> have music lessons
> ~~eat a lot of sweets~~
> talk to his teacher about it
> buy expensive clothes
> go to bed late
> be nice to people

1 Gérard has got bad teeth. He
   shouldn't eat a lot of sweets
   ----------------------------------- .

2 Wendy doesn't have many
   friends. She -----------------------

   ----------------------------------- .

3 Franco doesn't have much
   money. He -----------------------

   ----------------------------------- .

4 Adriana wants to be a singer.
   She -----------------------------

   ----------------------------------- .

5 Julia is always tired when she
   gets up. She -----------------------

   ----------------------------------- .

6 Phil doesn't understand his
   Maths work. He -----------------------

   ----------------------------------- .

Look after yourself!

1 You _____ go to bed early before an exam.
2 You _____ eat plenty of fresh fruit and vegetables.
3 You _____ stand under a tree in a storm.
4 You _____ look left and right before crossing the road.

c Put the words in order to complete the questions. Then write answers about the customs in your country.

1 you What say should
   What should you say when you meet someone for the first time?
   You should say -----------------------------------

2 bow students Should
   --- when a teacher comes
   into the classroom?
   ----

3 present bring Should you a
   --- if someone invites you
   to their home?
   ----

4 you use should When
   --- someone's first name?
   ----

5 take Should off people
   --- their shoes when
   they go into your house?
   ----

d What do you think these people should/shouldn't do?
Write sentences, starting with *You*, *He*, *She* or *They*.

1 I can't talk to my friend because she's in San Francisco.
You should write her a letter.

2 Amy feels ill today.
She

3 I want to speak really good English.
You

4 I've got a Science test tomorrow.

5 Dave wants to travel to a different country.

6 I want a really good job when I leave school.

7 Alex has got a problem – he hasn't got any money.

8 Lucy and Amy want to have a big celebration for Dave's birthday.

2 Vocabulary

Personality adjectives

a Look at the pictures. Complete the words to describe the people.

1 *d i s o r g a n i s e d*   2 c _ _ _ _ r _ _ _ l   3 _ _ _ a _ _ _ _

4 _ _ _ _ l _ _ e   5 m _ _ _ _ _ _ b _ _ _ _   6 _ _ _ _ d-w _ _

7 _ _ _ g _ _ _ _ _ _ d   8 r _ _ _ _ _ _   9 n _ _ _ _ _ _ _ _ s

b 🔊 Listen to Dave talking about some of the students in his class. Underline the adjective that describes each person.

James	a	hard-working	b	cheerful	c	polite
Sally	a	honest	b	kind	c	friendly
Cathy	a	relaxed	b	polite	c	honest
Joanne	a	helpful	b	unkind	c	lazy
Max	a	dishonest	b	unfriendly	c	rude

3 Pronunciation
Silent consonants

a 🔊 Listen to the word pairs. In one of the two words, the consonant in brackets is silent. (Circle) the silent consonant. Then listen again, check and repeat.

1	answer	twenty	(w)
2	kind	knife	(k)
3	often	faster	(t)
4	autumn	station	(n)
5	climber	robber	(b)
6	horse	hour	(h)
7	went	wrong	(w)
8	hold	should	(l)
9	Science	disco	(c)

(In "answer" the w is circled.)

b 🔊 Here are some new words, each with a silent consonant. Which do you think is the silent letter, and how do you think you should pronounce the word? Listen, check and repeat.

1 lamb
2 could
3 kneel
4 column
5 wrap

4 Grammar
What's it like?

a Read the answers and write questions with *What (be) ... like?* Use the words in the box.

the weather   your new sunglasses   the party
your neighbour   ~~the film~~   Helen's friends

1 A: *What was the film like* ?

   B: It was great. It was really exciting and the computer effects were amazing.

2 A: _____ ?

   B: Well, they're a sort of blue colour and I think they're cool.

3 A: _____ ?

   B: It's cloudy and very cold. They say it's going to snow later.

4 A: _____ ?

   B: They were OK. They were quite friendly and some of them were interesting.

5 A: _____ ?

   B: I didn't enjoy it much. It was too crowded and the music was awful.

6 A: _____ ?

   B: Oh, she's nice. She's really kind and friendly.

b Now answer these questions about you.

1 What's your best friend like?
2 What are your favourite shoes like?
3 What was your first teacher like?

5 Vocabulary
Adjectives for expressing opinions

a Match the adjectives that have similar meanings.

1	boring	a	dreadful
2	brilliant	b	good
3	awful	c	dull
4	cool	d	fantastic

b Underline the correct adjectives.

1. What's that book like?
   It's OK, but it's a bit *dull/cool*.

2. What's your new jacket like?
   It's *awful/brilliant*! I love it.

3. You should buy these.
   No, I think they're *attractive/ugly*.

4. Are you enjoying this programme?
   No, it isn't very *boring/interesting*.

6 Culture in mind

Complete the sentences with the words in the box.

> You're welcome   Pardon   Can I have
> Thank you   please

1. .... six oranges, please?

2. A: You should wait in the queue.
   B: .... ?
   A: I said: you should wait in the queue.

3. A: Thanks very much.
   B: ....

4. I'd like a black coffee, ...

5. A: I bought you a little present.
   B: Oh, great! ....

7 Study help
Vocabulary

It's a good idea to group adjectives with their opposites in your Vocabulary notebook.

a Find another pair of personality adjectives to add to each list.

b Find the opposites of the adjectives in the box and write them in the lists.
Use your dictionary if you need to.

> healthy   orderly   beautiful   obedient
> usual   quiet   lucky   stupid

dis-
honest – dishonest
....
....

un-
kind – unkind
....
....
....
....

Different adjective
hard-working – lazy
....
....
....
....

c Can you find the opposites to add to these lists? Use your dictionary to help you.

> useful   possible   perfect   careful

im-
probable – improbable
....
....

-less
powerful – powerless
....
....

Skills in mind

8 Read

Jacqueline is from France. After she left school, she spent three months studying in England. Read her article giving advice to language students. Mark the statements *T* (true) or *F* (false) and correct the false statements.

I went abroad for the first time when I was 18. I travelled to England to study English, but I didn't learn to speak well. The main problem was that I made friends with other French people, so I spent too much time speaking French. It's important to make English friends and to spend a lot of time with your English host family. If they have young children, it's even better. The children in my host family were great teachers.

Another problem was that I was worried about making mistakes when I spoke, so I didn't say much. But you shouldn't worry.

English people are usually polite and helpful. You can't learn to say things if you don't talk. You should leave your dictionary at home and say what you can.

To help your listening, try to understand the conversations of English people in shops and on buses. I heard some very interesting things! Listening isn't easy at the beginning, but don't give up!

Read a newspaper and watch the news on TV every day. All the students in my class did this, and it helped a lot. Of course, the cinema is a fun way to practise your English. And listening to songs is helpful, too – there are lots of good British bands.

Finally, don't study too hard. Give yourself lots of time for fun, but try to have fun the English way.

Reading tip
Answering true/false *questions*

- Read the statements very carefully – it's important to know exactly what they are saying before you decide if they are true or false. Underline key words and phrases. Also look out for negatives – if you miss these, you will get the wrong answers.

- Read the examples. Why are they true or false? Look through the text to find the parts that give the answers ('I went abroad for the first time when I was 18', 'I didn't learn to speak well'). Look out for expressions that are similar in meaning (for example, 'go to other countries' – 'went abroad'). Continue this close reading when you are deciding if the other statements are true or false.

- This exercise also asks you to correct the false statements. (You don't have to write anything when the statement is true.) Look at the example correction for statement 2 and see how it uses information from the text.

- Make sure you are only correcting the false information. Don't write more than you need to.

1 Jacqueline didn't go to other countries when she was a young child.　　　　　　　　　　　　　　　 ☐ *T*

---

2 She spoke good English after her three months in England.　☐ *F*
She didn't learn to speak well.

---

3 She had a lot of English friends.　　　　　　　　　　　 ☐

---

4 The children in her English family didn't help her.　　　 ☐

---

5 She thinks students should always carry a dictionary with them.　☐

---

6 She listened to English people talking when she went shopping.　☐

---

7 She thinks it's a good idea to watch TV every day.　　　 ☐

---

8 She believes students should always study very hard.　　 ☐

9 Write

Use Jacqueline's advice to make a poster.

GOING ABROAD TO STUDY ENGLISH? REMEMBER THIS ADVICE!

YOU SHOULD ...
spend a lot of time with your host family.

YOU SHOULDN'T ...
make friends only with people from your country.

Unit check

1 Fill in the spaces

Complete the dialogue with the words in the box.

> dishonest   should   miserable   kind   ~~nervous~~   disorganised   shouldn't   lazy   cheerful   like

A: The exams are in two days' time, but Gino isn't __nervous__ at all.

B: I know – he's amazing. He's always relaxed and [1]_____ , so he never stops smiling. Even when bad things happen he doesn't get [2]_____ .

A: Julie thinks he's [3]_____ . She says he never does any work.

B: That isn't true. You [4]_____ listen to Julie. She's often [5]_____ so you can't believe half the things she says.

A: You know Gino's brother, don't you? What's he [6]_____ ?

B: Well, he's incredibly [7]_____ – he's always late and he's always losing things. But he's very [8]_____ – he thinks about people and does a lot to help them. You [9]_____ meet him. He's a nice guy.

[9]

2 Choose the correct answers

Circle the correct answers, a, b or c.

1 He was _____ . He really hurt my feelings.
   a (unkind)   b nervous   c friendly

2 I'm sure her story is true. She's a very _____ person.
   a rude   b hard-working   c honest

3 Our neighbours never speak to us. They're very _____ .
   a miserable   b lazy   c unfriendly

4 You're going to love this music. It's _____ .
   a dreadful   b brilliant   c attractive

5 The party was _____ and boring.
   a dull   b cool   c ugly

6 You _____ wear those jeans. They're too short.
   a must   b should   c shouldn't

7 That bike isn't very safe. I don't think he _____ ride it.
   a should   b must   c shouldn't

8 _____ buy this book for Dad's birthday?
   a We should   b Should we   c Do we should

9 A: _____ the weather like? B: It's awful!
   a What was   b What's   c What does

[8]

3 Correct the mistakes

In each sentence there is a mistake with *should/shouldn't* or with *What's it like?*
Underline the mistake and write the correct sentence.

1 Lesley should <u>seeing</u> a doctor. *Lesley should see a doctor.*

2 They shouldn't to talk loudly in the library. _____

3 I don't think you shouldn't go out without a coat. _____

4 What your new teachers are like? _____

5 We should to get up early tomorrow. _____

6 He doesn't should smoke when people are eating. _____

7 Do I should send an email to Martin? _____

8 You shouldn't be lazy, do you? _____

9 What's the concert like last night? _____

[8]

How did you do?

Total: [25]

| 😊 | Very good 20 – 25 | 😐 | OK 14 – 19 | 😟 | Review Unit 6 again 0 – 13 |

7 How brave!

1 Remember and check

Match the questions with the answers, and then complete the answers with the verbs in the box. Check with the text on page 46.

| are scared | will kill | didn't hit |
| take it back | picked it up |

1 Why did the woman drive to the forest with the baby gorilla?
2 The woman was really worried. What did she think?
3 The gorilla wanted to scare the woman. What did it do?
4 What happened to the baby gorilla?
5 Is it true that gorillas are very dangerous to people?

a She thought, 'I hope the mother will recognise the baby. If not, perhaps she _____ it.'

b No, not normally. Gorillas will only attack you if you show that you _____ .

c The big gorilla walked over to it, _____ and moved away.

d The baby was well again. The woman had to _____ to its family.

e It lifted its hand, but it _____ her.

2 Grammar

First conditional

a Underline the correct words.

1 If *you finish / you'll finish* work before five, Olga will take you home in her car.
2 They'll be disappointed if they *don't / won't* get concert tickets.
3 If Alan wants to have a shower, *he has to / he'll have to* hurry.
4 If you don't wear a coat, *you're / you'll be* cold.
5 If Chris doesn't phone Sue tonight, *she sends / she'll send* him an email.

b Write first conditional sentences.

1 If / Judith / miss / bus, / she / be / miserable

_____

2 If / train / not come soon, / we / walk home

_____

3 You / not get wet / if you / wear / raincoat

_____

4 I / not sing well / at concert / if I / be / too nervous

_____

5 If / my friends / see me, / they / not recognise / me

_____

c The pictures show people's possible plans for Saturday. Complete the conditional sentences.

Christina

Colin

1 If the weather is nice, Christina _____

2 If it _____

3 If Colin _____

4 If he _____

d Think about your next free afternoon or evening, or your next weekend. Write three true sentences using the first conditional.

1 If ....

2 If ....

3 .... if ....

e Look at the pictures and complete the sentence. Use *will* or *won't* and the words in brackets.

1 If he tries to climb up, ...
.... (break)

2 If she goes into the garden, ...
.... (attack her)

3 If we keep quiet, ...
.... (find us)

4 If they drive too fast, ...
.... (crash)

5 If you go to bed, ...
.... (feel better)

6 If the weather gets worse, ...
.... (take off)

when and *if*

f Complete the sentences with *when* or *if*.

1 Neil will look for a job ....
the summer holidays begin.

2 I'll do my homework ....
I get home.

3 We'll take a taxi .... Dad
can't meet us at the station.

4 .... you waste time, you
won't finish your work.

5 It'll be great .... I win this
competition!

6 We'll have a big celebration
.... you turn 21.

3 Pronunciation

Sentence stress

(a) 🔊 Listen to the sentences from the text in Unit 7.
<u>Underline</u> the stressed words/syllables. Then listen again and repeat.

1   If the mother doesn't recognise the baby, she won't take it back.
2   They only attack when you show you're scared.
3   If I turn and run away, this gorilla will attack me.
4   But if I don't move, he'll go away.

(b) 🔊 <u>Underline</u> the stressed words/syllables in the sentences in Exercise 2f.
Then listen, check and repeat.

4 Vocabulary

Adjectives of feeling

(a) Match the two parts of the sentences.

1   My dog gets frightened
2   Rosa's parents were annoyed
3   She was tired
4   I was interested
5   She's bored with her job,
6   My little sister is getting excited

a   and I think she should look for a new one.
b   about her birthday party next weekend.
c   when she hears fireworks.
d   after her long walk in the mountains.
e   because she was late home from the party.
f   when I heard that Matt is going out with Carol.

(b) Complete the sentences with the adjectives in the box.

> annoyed   exciting   frightening   worried   interesting   terrified

1   This book isn't very _____ .
2   We can't find our cat. I'm _____ about him.
3   It was a very _____ match.
4   I'm _____ of snakes.
5   Our teacher gets _____ when we don't listen.
6   There were strange noises in the night. It was _____ .

Verbs

c Look at the pictures and fill in the verbs. If you need help, look at Exercise 7 on page 49.

1 ....

2 ....

3 ....

4 ....

5 ....

6 ....

7 ....

5 Everyday English

Complete the dialogue. Use a word or phrase from each box.

No	Hang		~~I know~~	deal
~~How should~~	No big		way	on

Tom: Do you know who I dreamed about last night?

Susie: No. *How should I know* ?

Tom: Well, it was you! I dreamed that you asked me out and we went to the cinema together.

Susie: That's an idea. Maybe I should ask ...

Tom: So you're going to ask me out? Great. We can go to the cinema and after that ...

Susie: ¹ .... ! What are you talking about?

Tom: Didn't you ask me to go out with you?

Susie: Me? Ask you out? ² .... !

Tom: But you said ...

Susie: Oh, Tom. Not you – *Danny*. I want to ask Danny to go out with me.

Tom: Ah. Oh well, OK.

³ ....

6 Study help

Grammar

Here are some things you can do to help you remember and revise grammar.

- In your notebook, write down the grammar rule in the form of a diagram or summary. For example:

First conditional

If + present simple,	+	will

will	+	if + present simple

- Write example sentences which show the meaning clearly.

- Identify areas where you sometimes make mistakes. In your examples, highlight the difficult area with different coloured pens or highlighter pens.

- Go over the exercises in the Student's Book and Workbook.

- Record example sentences and listen to them from time to time, for example, when you are washing up or on your way to school.

- Work with a friend. Write some sentences on a particular grammar point and include one grammar mistake in each sentence. Exchange your work and correct the mistakes in your friend's sentences. Then discuss the sentences together.

Choose some or all of these points and use them for revising the first conditional.

Skills in mind

7 Read

a Read the school newspaper article and put the pictures in the correct order. Write 1–5 in the boxes.

A medal for bravery

One of our students received a medal yesterday at Macclesfield Town Hall for her bravery in helping an elderly lady.

Sharon Armstrong, 15, was in Lyme Park in Stockport last May when she saw a pit-bull terrier which was barking furiously at an elderly woman, Mrs Anne Phillips. Mrs Phillips called for help, so Sharon ran closer and picked up some stones from the path.

'I started to throw stones at the dog,' Sharon told us. 'Then it turned round and began to come towards me. I was really scared. I stood still and shouted at the dog and it stopped, but it kept barking and it looked very angry. I thought it was going to attack me.'

At that moment, however, the dog's owner, Mr Paul Ashcroft, arrived and called the dog off.

'Sharon is a very brave girl,' commented Mr Thomson, the mayor of Macclesfield, when he gave Sharon her medal. But Sharon says, 'I don't really think I did anything special. The lady was clearly very frightened, so I just did the first thing I could think of.'

Mr Ashcroft was fined £100 for not keeping his dog on a lead.

b Answer the questions.

1 Who did the dog bark at first? ....

2 What did Sharon throw at the dog? ....

3 What did the dog do next? ....

4 Why didn't the dog attack Sharon? ....

8 Write

Write a newspaper report about a person / people who did something brave. It can be about a true event or you can invent one.

Writing tip

Organising a newspaper report

Look again at the text. Notice that in the first paragraph of the report, the writer identifies the time and makes a very short summary of the event. The report then gives a fuller description of the event with comments from Sharon and other people.

Follow the same pattern when you write your report. Think out the details before you begin to write. Make notes on these questions:

- Who was there?
- Where and when did it happen?
- What happened first?
- What happened next?
- Who said something about it?

Unit check

1 Fill in the spaces

Complete the message with the words in the box.

> I'm   I'll   tired   ~~interesting~~   interested   annoying   arrives   exciting   bored   when

How are you? Nothing _____*interesting*_____ is happening here and I'm feeling [1]_____
– there's nothing to do! I started watching the tennis on TV but it wasn't very [2]_____ and
I stopped watching. I can't go out because I have to look after my little brother. It's [3]_____ ,
because I had plans to go shopping with Louise this afternoon. Dad's at home, but he had to work all night
in his job, so he's very [4]_____ now. Anyway, I can go out later [5]_____ Mum
is home. If you're still [6]_____ in seeing the new Spielberg film, [7]_____ come
with you. If Mum [8]_____ early, I'll meet you at the café at six. But if [9]_____
not there, I'll see you at the cinema before the film starts. Is that OK?

`9`

2 Choose the correct answers

(Circle) the correct answers, a, b or c.

1 I think it's a very _____ book.
   a interest   b interested   c (interesting)
2 Don't be _____ . You're quite safe.
   a frighten   b frightened   c frightening
3 It's a dangerous situation, but we must try to keep _____ .
   a brave   b tired   c calm
4 Our car crashed and overturned.
   It was _____ .
   a boring   b terrifying   c annoying

5 The bank _____ took £20,000.
   a robbers   b fighters   c jumpers
6 If the rope _____ , you'll fall.
   a breaks   b will break   c won't break
7 If they hire a car, _____ to Spain.
   a they drive   b they'll drive   c they drove
8 The dog won't attack him if _____ move.
   a he'll   b he won't   c he doesn't
9 We'll feel more relaxed _____ the exams finish.
   a if   b when   c because

`8`

3 Correct the mistakes

In each sentence there is a mistake with the first conditional or with *when* and *if*.
Underline the mistake and write the correct sentence.

1 If the fire gets worse, this building <u>collapses</u>. *If the fire gets worse, this building will collapse.*

2 If you'll go to bed now, you'll wake up early tomorrow. _____

3 Sam is healthier if he eats more fruit. _____

4 Paula will sing well if she not gets nervous. _____

5 If it's rainy tomorrow, we don't go horse-riding. _____

6 You'll miss the bus when you don't run. _____

7 I stop writing to Jane if she doesn't answer my letters. _____

8 If Tim goes to university, he will becomes a lawyer. _____

9 If the winter comes, we will get some snow. _____

`8`

How did you do?

Total: `25`

| 🙂 | Very good 20 – 25 | 😐 | OK 14 – 19 | 🙁 | Review Unit 7 again 0 – 13 |

8 It's a mad world

1 Remember and check

a Match the sentence parts. Check with the text on page 52.

1	John Evans	grows	of bed.
2	The man from Scotland	has never had	things on his head.
3	The man from Thailand	balances	an accident.
4	Len Vale Onslow	never gets out	his hair.
5	Susan Smith	never cuts	onions.

b Complete the sentences.

1 My parents _____ sunflowers.

2 They're _____ of the car.

3 Put the knife down! You might _____ yourself!

4 This animal can _____ a ball on its nose.

2 Vocabulary

Animals

a Find ten names of animals in the wordsquare.

```
R I S N A K E D P E
F R I T P C J A D R
T A R A N T U L A M
A B Y T I D U L E O
L B S I O T P I K U
N I V G F R O G E S
O T C E T O S A N E
R C O R W N A T L D
E M W P A R R O T H
H A E L G H O R S E
```

b Complete the sentences.
Use eight of the animal words from Exercise 2a.

1 A _____ lives in Asia. It's a type of cat.

2 A _____ moves along the ground without any legs.

3 We get milk from a _____ .

4 A _____ has got eight legs.

5 An _____ lives in rivers and it eats meat.

6 A _____ is a bird. It usually has very bright colours.

7 A _____ moves by jumping or swimming.

8 A _____ eats plants and its home is under the ground.

c Write your own sentences for these animals.

1 dog _____

2 cat _____

3 horse _____

4 mouse _____

3 Grammar

Present perfect

a Complete the sentences. Use the past participle form of the verbs in the box.

play   eat   drive   listen   work   write
do   learn

1 Michael has often _____ tennis at the gym.

2 My mother has _____ in a lot of different jobs.

3 I've never _____ a car.

4 Liz has _____ how to fly a plane.

5 We've _____ Spanish food once or twice.

6 My cousins have never _____ a letter to me.

7 You've _____ to all my CDs.

8 Dad has always _____ the cooking at home.

b There is a mistake in each of these sentences. Underline the mistakes and correct them.

1 I'm read this book three times.

_____

_____

2 This actress has be in about 30 films.

_____

_____

3 Annette and Luke has never played ice hockey.

_____

_____

4 Martin hasn't spoke to my parents.

_____

_____

5 We never been in a helicopter.

_____

_____

6 You've travel to a lot of countries.

_____

_____

c Put the words in order to make questions and answers.

1 A: your Has father competition won ever a

   Has your father ever won a competition?

   B: won he's anything No, never

   No, he's never won anything.

2 A: ever snake you Has a bitten

   _____

   B: snake I've a No, never seen

   _____

3 A: flown to you Have America ever

   _____

   B: never in I've plane No, been a

   _____

4 A: in your swum this friends pool Have

   _____

   B: they've swim never to learned No,

   _____

d Use the words to write questions. Then write the short answer that is true for you.

1 see / a tiger?

   A: *Have you ever seen a tiger?*

   B: *Yes I have / No I haven't.*

2 meet / a pop star?

   A: _____

   B: _____

3 eat / Mexican food?

   A: _____

   B: _____

4 try / windsurfing?

   A: _____

   B: _____

5 be / in hospital?

   A: _____

   B: _____

e Complete the dialogue. Use the present perfect form of the verbs.

Lynne: Tony! I ^{1}_____ (never see) you looking so happy. Is this your new bike?

Tony: Yeah. Isn't it brilliant? I ^{2}_____ (never have) such a good bike before.

Lynne: Does it go well? ^{3}_____ you _____ (have) any problems with it?

Tony: No, it goes like a bird. Tell you what – why don't we go for a long ride, out to Moorsby Park?

Lynne: Moorsby Park? I ^{4}_____ (never be) there.

Tony: Oh, it's really nice. Dad and I ^{5}_____ (drive) there a few times in the car. It's about 20 kilometres from here.

Lynne: Wow! I ^{6}_____ (never cycle) that far.

Tony: Don't worry, a little bike ride ^{7}_____ (never kill) anyone! We'll be back by lunch time. And then we can go and get some food at the Mexican take-away place. We can have nachos. ^{8}_____ you _____ (ever eat) nachos?

Lynne: Yeah, lots of times. I love them. OK, then – let's go!

f 🔊 Listen again to part of the interview with Mr Brown from page 53. Fill in each space with three words.

Interviewer: So have you ever had any problems yourself? Some of these animals are dangerous, aren't they?

Mr Brown: Well, the tarantulas ^{1}_____ _____ _____ once or twice.

Interviewer: What do your neighbours think about all these animals?

Mr Brown: Well, ^{2}_____ _____ _____ .

Interviewer: Have any of your ^{3}_____ _____ _____ ?

Mr Brown: Yes. The parrot escaped in 1998. But the alligator and the tarantulas ^{4}_____ _____ _____ .

4 Pronunciation

Present perfect

🔊 Listen and tick the sentence you hear. Then listen again and repeat.

1 I cut my finger.
  I've cut my finger.

2 Did you see the parrot?
  Have you seen the parrot?

3 He spoke to my mother.
  He's spoken to my mother.

4 They won lots of prizes.
  They've won lots of prizes.

5 He's seeing the doctor.
  He's seen the doctor.

6 She's eating the chocolate.
  She's eaten the chocolate.

5 Vocabulary

Verb and noun pairs

Complete the sentences. Use a word from each box.

raise	win	break	told	took

the record	a risk	a joke	a prize	money

1 We should enter the competition. We might _____ .

2 You _____ when you went skating on the river. The ice is quite thin.

3 It's a charity concert. They want to _____ for the Red Cross.

4 She's training hard and her times are excellent. She's sure to win the 800 metres race, and she also hopes to _____ .

5 I _____ , but nobody laughed.

6 Culture in mind

a Fill in the puzzle. If you need help, check with the text on page 56.

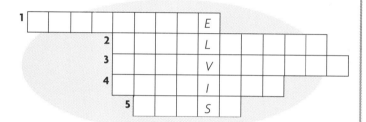

```
1 [ ][ ][ ][ ][ ][ ][ ][E][ ]
      2 [ ][ ][ ][ ][L][ ][ ][ ]
      3 [ ][ ][ ][V][ ][ ][ ][ ][ ]
      4 [ ][ ][ ][I][ ][ ]
           5 [ ][ ][S][ ][ ][ ]
```

b Mark the statements *T* (true) or *F* (false). Check with the text.

1 *Heartbreak Hotel* is the place where Elvis died. ☐

2 One of his hit songs was *The King*. ☐

3 Nobody has sold more records than Elvis. ☐

4 Elvis didn't live at Graceland. ☐

5 Some people don't believe that Elvis is dead. ☐

6 Some Elvis look-alikes have their own fans. ☐

7 Study help

Grammar

For irregular verbs, learn the past participle together with the past simple form. It's a good idea to divide the verbs into groups:

Base form	Past simple	Past participle
No change		
put	put	put
....	....	....

Same past simple and past participle		
Base form	Past simple	Past participle
have	had	had
....	....	....
....	....	....

Different past participle		
Base form	Past simple	Past participle
speak	spoke	spoken
....	....	....
....	....	....
....	....	....
....	....	....
....		....

Write the three forms of these verbs in the correct lists.

write	fly	make	cut	break	meet
drive	go				

Keep lists like this in your notebook and add to them. Go through your lists regularly and say the three verb forms aloud. You can also record them and listen to them regularly.

Skills in mind

8 Read and listen

🔊 Here are two jokes. Read and listen, and fill in the spaces.

1 A man goes into a pizza place and asks for a pizza. The girl asks him what he wants on it.

'Oh, ham and ¹ _____ and olives, please.'

'Fine,' says the girl. 'And what size pizza ² _____ _____ _____?'

'What sizes have you got?' asks the man.

'Well, you can have small, medium or large.'

'Oh,' says the man. 'Um ... medium, ³ _____.'

The girl says: 'OK. And do you want me to ⁴ _____ it into ⁵ _____ pieces or ⁶ _____ pieces?

The man thinks about it and says, 'Just four pieces, please. I'm not really very hungry. I don't think I ⁷ _____ _____ _____ _____ !'

2 Two farmers go out one day and they buy two horses, one each. They put the two horses in a field.

'Wait a minute,' says one farmer. 'How will we know which horse is yours and which horse is ⁸ _____?'

So the two farmers sit down and think about it. They ⁹ _____ to paint the horses' tails – one tail will be ¹⁰ _____ and the other tail will be

¹¹ _____ .

But that night, it ¹² _____ and the paint comes off. So the two farmers think about it again. Then one of them says, 'Oh, what stupid farmers we are! Look, it's easy. Your ¹³ _____ _____ is ¹⁴ _____ _____ my

¹⁵ _____ _____ !'

9 Write

Write a funny story.
It can be:

- something that really happened to you or someone you know
- a joke that you can tell
- something that happened in a film or a book
- a story that you make up yourself.

Try to plan your story so that the funniest part comes at the end.

Unit 5

be going to: intentions

1   We use *be going to* to talk about things we intend to do in the future.

   I'm going to visit my grandfather at the weekend.
   Marco is going to buy some new jeans tomorrow.
   Our neighbours are going to sell their house next year.

2   The form is the present simple of *be* + *going to* + base form of the verb.

   I'm going to stay at home on Sunday.   *I'm not going to play football.*
   We're going to leave early tomorrow.   *We aren't going to be late.*
   She's going to do some shopping.   *She isn't going to spend much money.*

3   The question is formed with the present simple of *be* + subject + *going to* + base form of the verb.

   Are you going to watch the film tonight?   *Yes, I am. / No, I'm not.*
   Is Paul going to meet you after school?   *Yes, he is. / No, he isn't.*
   Are your parents going to buy a car?   *Yes, they are. / No, they aren't.*
   How are you going to get home?
   When is she going to learn to drive?

be going to: predictions

We can also use **be going to** to make predictions based on things we know or can see.

   Look at the clouds. It's going to rain soon.
   Silvana didn't ring her parents. They're going to be angry with her.
   It's 10.30 now. You aren't going to finish your homework this evening.

must/mustn't

1   *Must* is similar to *have to*. We use it to say that it is necessary or very important to do something.

   You must come home before 11 o'clock.
   I'm late – I must go!

2   We use *mustn't* to say that it is necessary or very important not to do something.

   You mustn't be late.
   I mustn't forget to go to the bank.

   Mustn't has a different meaning from *don't/ doesn't have to*.

   You don't have to leave now. (= It isn't necessary for you to leave, although you can if you want to.)
   You mustn't leave now. (= Don't go – you must stay here!)

3   *Must* is a modal, like *will* (see Unit 11). We use *must/mustn't* + base form of the verb, and the form is the same for all subjects. We don't use any form of *do* in the negative.

   I must get up early tomorrow.   *I mustn't miss the train.*
   She must save some money.   *She mustn't spend it all.*
   You must be quiet in the library.   *You mustn't make a noise.*

Unit 6

should/shouldn't

1 When we want to say that something is a good idea (or is not a good idea), we can use *should* or *shouldn't*.

You **should see** a doctor.   (I think this is a good idea for you.)
I **should work** this evening.   (I think this is a good idea for me.)
They **shouldn't buy** that computer.   (I think this is a bad idea for them.)
Should we **go** home now?   (Do you think this is a good idea for us?)

2 *Should* is another modal, like *will* and *must*. We use *should/shouldn't* + base form of the verb, and the form is the same for all subjects. We don't use any form of *do* in the negative.

I **should lose** some weight.   I **shouldn't eat** this chocolate.
You **should come** to the cinema with us.   You **shouldn't stay** at home on your own.
Mike **should practise** the guitar every day.   He **shouldn't give up** his music lessons.

3 Questions are formed with *will* + subject + base form of the verb. Again, we don't use any form of *do* in questions or short answers.

Should we **wait** for Lisa?   Yes, we **should**. / No, we **shouldn't**.
Should I **tell** my parents?   Yes, you **should**. / No, you **shouldn't**.

What's it like?

1 We use a form of the question *What's it like?* if we want to hear a description or opinion of something/somebody. The answer to this question will often contain adjectives.

What's she **like**?   She's an interesting person and she's very intelligent.
What are your neighbours **like**?   They're OK. They're polite but they're not very friendly.

2 The question is formed with *What + be +* subject *+ like*? The word *like* doesn't change – it is quite different from the verb *like*.

What's the weather **like** today?
What are those cakes **like**?
What was the film **like** last night?
Did you meet Helen's cousins? **What were** they **like**?

Unit 7

First conditional

1 In conditional sentences there are two clauses, an *if* clause and a result clause. We use the first conditional when it is possible or likely that the situation in the *if* clause will happen in the future.

If I pass the test, my parents **will be** happy. (= It's possible that I'll pass, but I'm not sure.)

If it doesn't rain, we'll go for a walk. (= Perhaps it won't rain, but I'm not sure.)

2 The *if* clause is formed with *If* + subject + present simple. The result clause is formed with subject + *will* + base form of the verb. There is a comma after the *if* clause.

If he sees Martina, **he'll tell** her about the party.
If we have time, **we'll do** some shopping at the supermarket.
If this programme isn't interesting, **I'll watch** a video.
If you don't start your homework soon, **you won't finish** it tonight.

3 We can change the order of the two clauses. In this case, there is no comma between the clauses.

He'll tell Martina about the party **if he sees** her.
We'll do some shopping at the supermarket **if we have** time.

when and if

If indicates a possible situation. If we use *when* instead of *if*, it indicates that we are sure that the situation is going to happen.

If *he sees Martina, he'll tell her about the party.* *(= Perhaps he'll see her, perhaps not.)*

When *he sees Martina, he'll tell her about the party.* *(= He's going to see her — this will definitely happen.)*

Unit 8

Present perfect + *ever/never*

1 We often use the present perfect to talk about things from the beginning of our life until now.

John **has travelled** *to lots of different countries.* *(= from when he was born until now)*

I **haven't met** *your brother.* *(= at any time in my life, from when I was born until now)*

They've always **lived** *in this town.* *(= from when they were born until now)*

2 When we use the present perfect with this meaning, we often use *ever* (= at any time in someone's life) in questions, and *never* (= not ever) in sentences.

Have *you* **ever eaten** *seafood?*

Has *Steve* **ever won** *a prize in a competition?*

I've **never been** *interested in music.*

She's **never tried** *to cook.*

3 The present perfect is formed with the present tense of *have* + past participle of the main verb.

For regular verbs, the past participle has the same *ed* ending as the past simple.
Irregular verbs have different past participles.

Regular verbs	**Irregular verbs**
*We've stay**ed** in Athens three times.*	*We've **been** there three times.*
*Julia hasn't us**ed** a computer.*	*She hasn't **written** any emails.*
*He's never play**ed** basketball.*	*He's never **driven** a car.*
*Have they ever climb**ed** a mountain?*	*Have they ever **flown** in a plane?*

For the past participles of irregular verbs, see the list on page 138 of the Student's Book.

4 Present perfect questions are formed with *have/has* + subject + past participle.

Have *they* **tried** *Japanese food?*   *Yes, they* **have**. */ No, they* **haven't**.
Have *you ever* **seen** *a snake?*   *Yes, I* **have**. */ No, I* **haven't**.
Has *he ever* **had** *a job?*   *Yes, he* **has**. */ No, he* **hasn't**.

✳ Wordlist

(v) = verb   (n) = noun   (adj) = adjective

Unit 1

Language learning

accent (n) /'æksənt/
communicate (v)
   /kə'mjuːnɪkeɪt/
correct (v, adj) /kə'rekt/
course (n) /kɔːs/
guess (v) /ges/
imitate (v) /'ɪmɪteɪt/
look up (v) /lʊk 'ʌp/
make mistakes (v)
   /meɪk mɪ'steɪks/
mean (v) /miːn/
mother tongue (n) /'mʌðər
   tʌŋ/
penfriend (n) /'penfrend/
practise (v) /'præktɪs/
pronounce (v) /prə'naʊns/
pronunciation (n)
   /prə,nʌnsi'eɪʃən/
speak (v) /spiːk/
translate (v) /trænz'leɪt/
translation (n)
   /trænz'leɪʃən/
wrong (adj) /rɒŋ/

Verbs

marry /'maeri/

Adjectives

best /best/
better /'betər/
boring /'bɔːrɪŋ/
cool /kuːl/
easy /'iːzi/
friendly /'frendli/
further/farther
   /'fɜːðər/, /'fɑːðər/
good-looking /,gʊd'lʊkɪŋ/
handsome /'hænsəm/
important /ɪm'pɔːtənt/
intelligent /ɪn'telɪdʒənt/
nice /naɪs/
normal /'nɔːməl/
popular /'pɒpjələr/
successful /sək'sesfəl/
talented /'tæləntɪd/
unusual /ʌn'juːʒəl/
worse /wɜːs/

Everyday English

Ace! /eɪs/
Cool! /kuːl/
Groovy! /'gruːvi/
Hip! /hɪp/
Neat! /niːt/
Wicked! /'wɪkɪd/

Unit 2

Future time expressions

day after tomorrow
   /'deɪ ,ɑːftər tə,mɒrəʊ/
in three days' time /ɪn θriː
   deɪz taɪm/
next (week/Saturday)
   /nekst/
tomorrow /tə'mɒrəʊ/
week (month) after next
   /'wiːk ɑːftər nekst/

Holidays

activity (n) /æk'tɪvəti/
adventure holiday (n)
   /əd'ventʃər 'hɒlədeɪ/
backpack (n) /'bækpæk/
bed and breakfast (n)
   /bed ənd 'brekfəst/
camping (n) /'kæmpɪŋ/
campsite (n) /'kæmpsaɪt/
canal boat (n) /kə'næl
   bəʊt/
canoeing (n) /kə'nuːɪŋ/
coach (n) /kəʊtʃ/
coast /kəʊst/
farm /fɑːm/
ferry (n) /'feri/
hiking (n) /'haɪkɪŋ/
hire (v) /haɪər/
horse-riding (n)
   /'hɔːsraɪdɪŋ/
houseboat (n) /'haʊsbəʊt/
island (n) /'aɪlənd/
kayak (n) /'kaɪæk/
mountain bike (n)
   /'maʊntɪn baɪk/
nature (n) /'neɪtʃər/
on horseback (adv) /ɒn
   'hɔːsbæk/
postcard (n) /'pəʊskɑːd/
sailing (n) /'seɪlɪŋ/
sightseeing (n) /'saɪtsiːɪŋ/
snorkelling (n) /'snɔːkəlɪŋ/

souvenir (n) /,suːvən'ɪər/
summer camp (n)
   /'sʌmər kæmp/
sunbathing (n) /'sʌnbeɪðɪŋ/
surfboard (n) /'sɜːfbɔːd/
tourist (n) /'tɔːrɪst/
valley /'væliː/
windsurfing (n)
   /'wɪnsɜːfɪŋ/
youth hostel (n) /'juːθ
   ,hɒstəl/

Unit 3

Verbs

crash /kræʃ/
float /fləʊt/
get married /get 'mærid/
have children /hæv
   'tʃɪldrən/
relax /rɪ'læks/

Nouns

bill /bɪl/
fortune cookie
   /'fɔːtʃuːn ,kʊki/
galaxy /'gæləksi/
joke /dʒəʊk/
nonsense /'nɒnsəns/
planet /'plænɪt/
space /speɪs/
spaceship /'speɪsʃɪp/
universe /'juːnɪvɜːs/

Everyday English

Anything else?
   /,eniθɪŋ 'els/
How embarassing!
   /,haʊ ɪm'bærəsɪŋ/
I don't believe it!
   /aɪ ,dəʊnt bɪ'liːv ɪt/
(It's) nonsense
   /'nɒnsəns/
the best bit /ðə 'best bɪt/

Unit 4

The weather

avalanche (n) /'ævəlɑːnʃ/
cloudy (adj) /'klaʊdi/
foggy (adj) /'fɒgi/
hot /hɒt/

ice (n) /aɪs/
rain (n) /reɪn/
sunny (adj) /'sʌni/
warm (adj) /wɔːm/
windy (adj) /'wɪndi/

Verbs

break /breɪk/
give up /gɪv 'ʌp/
go on /gəʊ 'ɒn/
go wrong /gəʊ 'rɒŋ/
hit /hɪt/
hope to /'həʊp tʊ/
keep going /kiːp 'gəʊɪŋ/
lift /lɪft/
reach /riːtʃ/
stand up /stænd 'ʌp/
strengthen /'streŋθən/

Nouns

climber /'klaɪmər/
determination
   /dɪ,tɜːmɪ'neɪʃən/
immigrant /'ɪmɪgrənt/
painting /'peɪntɪŋ/
politics /'pɒlətɪks/
rope /rəʊp/

Adverbs

badly /'bædli/
bitterly (cold) /'bɪtəli/
carefully /'keəfəli/
fast /fɑːst/
gradually /'grædʒuəli/
hard /hɑːd/
heavily /'hevɪli/
loudly /'laʊdli/
luckily /'lʌkɪli/
quietly /'kwaɪətli/
slowly /'sləʊli/
well /wel/

Unit 5

Celebrations

birthday cake (n) /'bɜːθdeɪ
   keɪk/
celebrate (v) /'seləbreɪt/
fireworks (n) /'faɪəwɜːks/
New Year's Eve (Day) (n)
   /njuː jɪərz 'iːv/

Phrasal verbs

fall off /fɔːl 'ɒf/
get across /get əˈkrɒs/
give up (smoking)
   /gɪv ʌp/
go off /gəʊ 'ɒf/
go on /gəʊ 'ɒn/
keep up /kiːp 'ʌp/
stick to /ˈstɪk tuː/
take up /teɪk 'ʌp/
throw away /θrəʊ əˈweɪ/
work out (a problem) /wɜːk
   aʊt/

Verbs

be going to
   /bi 'gəʊɪŋ tuː/
have a shower
   /hæv ə 'ʃaʊəʳ/
must /mʌst/
record /reˈkɔːd/

Nouns

resolution /ˌrezəˈluːʃ°n/

Unit 6

Verbs

bow /baʊ/
kiss /kɪs/
reply /rɪˈplaɪ/
should /ʃʊd/
touch /tʌtʃ/

Nouns

custom /ˈkʌstəm/
leather /ˈleðəʳ/
queue /kjuː/
tip /tɪp/

Adjectives of personality

cheerful /ˈtʃɪəf°l/
dishonest /dɪˈsɒnɪst/
disorganised
   /dɪsˈɔːgənaɪzd/
dull /dʌl/
friendly /ˈfrendli/
funny /ˈfʌni/
hard-working
   /ˌhɑːdˈwɜːkɪŋ/
honest /ˈɒnɪst/
kind /kaɪnd/
lazy /ˈleɪzi/
miserable /ˈmɪzərəbl/
nervous /ˈnɜːvəs/
organised /ˈɔːgºnaɪzd/
relaxed /rɪˈlækst/
rude /ruːd/

unfriendly /ʌnˈfrendli/
unkind /ʌnˈkaɪnd/

Adjectives of opinion

attractive /əˈtræktɪv/
awful /ˈɔːf°l/
brilliant /ˈbrɪliənt/
boring /ˈbɔːrɪŋ/
dreadful /ˈdredf°l/
interesting /ˈɪntrəstɪŋ/
ugly /ˈʌgli/

Unit 7

Verbs

ask somebody out /ɑːsk
   ˌsʌmbədi 'aʊt/
burn /bɜːn/
can't stand /kɑːnt
   'stænd/
collapse /kəˈlæps/
drop /drɒp/
feel /fiːl/
frighten /ˈfraɪt°n/
keep calm /kiːp 'kɑːm/
might /maɪt/
overturn /ˈəʊvətɜːn/
recognise /ˈrekəgnaɪz/
show /ʃəʊ/

Nouns

danger /ˈdeɪndʒəʳ/
gorilla /gəˈrɪlə/
gun /gʌn/
shark /ʃɑːk/
situation /ˌsɪtjuˈeɪʃ°n/

Compound nouns

bank robber
   /ˈbæŋk ˌrɒbəʳ/
firefighter /ˈfaɪəʳˌfaɪtəʳ/
mountain climber
   /ˈmaʊntɪn ˌklaɪməʳ/
parachute jumper
   /ˈpærəʃuːt ˌdʒʌmpəʳ/
racing driver
   /ˈreɪsɪŋ ˌdraɪvəʳ/
underwater photographer
   /ˌʌndəwɔːtəʳ
   fəˈtɒgrəfəʳ/

Adjectives of feeling

annoyed /əˈnɔɪd/
annoying /əˈnɔɪɪŋ/
bored /bɔːʳd/
brave /breɪv/
calm /kɑːm/
excited /ɪkˈsaɪtɪd/

exciting /ɪkˈsaɪtɪŋ/
frightened /ˈfraɪt°nd/
frightening /ˈfraɪt°nɪŋ/
interested /ˈɪntrəstɪd/
interesting /ˈɪntrəstɪŋ/
terrified /ˈterəfaɪd/
tired /taɪəʳd/
tiring /ˈtaɪəʳɪŋ/

Everyday English

Hang on. /hæŋ 'ɒn/
How should I know?
   /haʊ ʃəd 'aɪ nəʊ/
No big deal.
   /ˈnəʊ bɪg 'diːl/
No way! /nəʊ 'weɪ/

Unit 8

Animals

alligator (n) /ˈælɪgeɪtəʳ/
cow (n) /kaʊ/
frog (n) /frɒg/
mouse (n) /maʊs/
parrot (n) /ˈpærət/
rabbit (n) /ˈræbɪt/
snake (n) /sneɪk/
tarantula (n) /təˈræntjələ/
tiger (n) /ˈtaɪgəʳ/

Verbs

bite /baɪt/
collect /kəˈlekt/
complain /kəmˈpleɪn/
seem /siːm/

Verb + noun pairs

break a record
   /breɪk ə 'rekɔːd/
build a house
   /bɪld ə 'haʊs/
raise money /reɪz 'mʌni/
take a risk /teɪk ə 'rɪsk/
tell a joke /tel ə 'dʒəʊk/
win a prize
   /wɪn ə 'praɪz/

Nouns

album /ˈælbəm/
anniversary /ˌænɪˈvɜːs°ri/
charity /ˈtʃærɪti/
collection /kəˈlekʃ°n/
death /deθ/
escape /ɪˈskeɪp/
fan /fæn/
fingernail /ˈfɪŋgəneɪl/
ghost /gəʊst/
head /hed/
hit /hɪt/
look-alike /ˈlʊkəlaɪk/

neighbour /ˈneɪbəʳ/
record /ˈrekɔːd/
sighting /ˈsaɪtɪŋ/
sky-diver /ˈskaɪˌdaɪvəʳ/
wheelchair /ˈwiːltʃeəʳ/
world record /wɜːld
   'rekɔːd/

Adjectives

mad /mæd/
middle-aged
   /ˌmɪdlˈeɪdʒd/
poor /pɔːʳ/

Irregular verbs and phonetics

Irregular verbs

Base form	Past simple	Past participle
be	was/were	been
beat	beat	beaten
become	became	become
begin	began	begun
bite	bit	bitten
break	broke	broken
build	built	built
buy	bought	bought
can	could	could
catch	caught	caught
choose	chose	chosen
come	came	come
cut	cut	cut
do	did	done
drive	drove	driven
eat	ate	eaten
fall	fell	fallen
feel	felt	felt
find	found	found
fly	flew	flown
get	got	got
give	gave	given
go	went	gone
grow	grew	grown
have	had	had
hear	heard	heard
hit	hit	hit
hurt	hurt	hurt
keep	kept	kept
know	knew	known
leave	left	left
lose	lost	lost
make	made	made
meet	met	met
put	put	put
read	read	read
ride	rode	ridden
run	ran	run
say	said	said
see	saw	seen
sell	sold	sold
send	sent	sent
sit	sat	sat
sleep	slept	slept
speak	spoke	spoken
stand	stood	stood
swim	swam	swum
take	took	taken
teach	taught	taught
tell	told	told
think	thought	thought
throw	threw	thrown
understand	understood	understood
wake	woke	woke
win	won	won
write	wrote	written

Phonetic symbols

Consonants

/p/	pen
/b/	be
/t/	two
/d/	do
/k/	can
/g/	good
/f/	five
/v/	very
/m/	make
/n/	nice
/ŋ/	sing
/s/	see
/z/	trousers
/w/	we
/l/	listen
/r/	right
/j/	you
/h/	he
/θ/	thing
/ð/	this
/ʃ/	she
/tʃ/	cheese
/ʒ/	usually
/dʒ/	German

Vowels

/æ/	man
/ɑː/	father
/e/	ten
/ɜː/	thirteen
/ə/	mother
/ɪ/	sit
/iː/	see
/ʊ/	book
/uː/	food
/ʌ/	up
/ɒ/	hot
/ɔː/	four

Diphthongs

/eɪ/	great
/aɪ/	fine
/ɔɪ/	boy
/ɪə/	hear
/eə/	chair
/aʊ/	town
/əʊ/	go
/ʊə/	pure

Acknowledgements

The publishers are grateful to the following for permission to reproduce photographic material:

Alamy p. 68(mr); Getty Image Bank p. 100; The Travel Library p. 68(tr).

All other photographs taken by Gareth Boden Photography.

The publishers are grateful to the following illustrators:

Mark Duffin, pp. 91, 109; Sophie Joyce, pp. 62, 80; Rob Loxston, pp. 81, 88, 106, 82; Stephen May, p. 84; Lee Montgomery, pp. 70, 72, 75, 94, 104, 90; Ken Oliver, c/o Wildlife Art, p. 102; Peters & Zabransky, p. 104; David Shenton, pp. 78, 84-85, 90, 96-97, 105, 108, 111-112; Kim Smith, c/o Eastwing Illustration Agency, pp. 73, 78, 85, 99, 110; Kath Walker, pp. 67, 92, 103; Darrell Warner, c/o Beehive Illustration, pp. 74, 110.

The publishers are grateful to the following contributors:

Sarah Ackroyd: CD-ROM exercises
Bee2 Ltd: multimedia developer
Gareth Boden: commissioned photography
Kevin Brown: picture research
Annie Cornford: editorial work
Fraser Symon: CD-ROM audio recording
Pentacorbig: text design and layouts
Anne Rosenfeld: audio CD audio recordings
Sally Smith: photographic direction

The publishers are grateful to Pilar Larcade for the photograph of horse-riding on the CD-ROM.

The CD-ROM photographs are from © Royalty-Free/CORBIS or taken by Cambridge University Press.

* Study notes

* Study notes

CD instructions

Audio CD
Play the CD in a standard CD player, or on your computer. To play it on your computer, insert the disc into your CD-ROM drive, and open your computer's CD player software (for example, Microsoft® Windows Media® Player). The CD-ROM application will open automatically – if you do not want to run the application, close or minimise it.

CD-ROM
No installation – simply insert the disc into your CD-ROM drive and the application will start automatically. Close any media applications (for example, Microsoft® Windows Media® Player) before inserting the disc. If the application does not start automatically, browse to your CD-ROM drive and double-click the 'EIM' icon.

Audio CD track listing

TRACK	UNIT	EXERCISE	TRACK	UNIT	EXERCISE
1	Introduction		12	5	4
2	1	4a	13	5	7
3	1	7	14	6	2b
4	2	4a	15	6	3a
5	2	4b	16	6	3b
6	2	8	17	7	3a
7	3	1a	18	7	3b
8	3	2a	19	8	3f
9	3	2b	20	8	4
10	4	6a	21	8	8
11	4	6b			